MEN AGAINST THE SEA

High Drama in the Atlantic

BY CYRIL ROBINSON

Cover by Ed McNally

LANCELOT PRESS

Windsor, Nova Scotia

To

Bev, Bobbie, and Cammy

Articles released through the courtesy of
Weekend Magazine.

PUBLISHED 1971
  First printing - June 1971
  Second printing - May 1972
LANCELOT PRESS LIMITED, Windsor, N. S.

CONTENTS

5

1

ORDEAL OF THE SHEILA PAT

A dense fog had begun to shroud the Nova Scotian coast as the trawler Sheila Patricia – better known in her home port of Mulgrave, N. S., as "the Pat" for short – plowed through heavy seas toward the fishing grounds.

The scene was about 40 miles off Green Island, N. S. The 159-ton, steel-hulled craft had put out from Mulgrave at 3 P. M. on Tuesday, April 29, with sufficient fuel oil for a 21-day trip.

It was now 11:30 A.M. next day. With luck, the vessel would be back in port within nine or 10 days with a good catch.

The wind was strong from the south and, although visibility was decreasing, better weather was forecast for the evening. There was nothing in the elements this day to unduly alarm Capt. Uriah "Lollie" Hillier or others of the vessel's 13-man crew. Just another routine trip to the fishing grounds, they thought.

In his cabin, the Pat's 38-year-old skipper, one of the seafaring Hilliers from Belloram, Nfld., eased his stout, stocky frame into a chair beside the ship's radio. Capt. Hillier busied himself with details of the trip and meanwhile kept close tabs on the weather. A devoted family man, he had left his wife and four children, aged five to 13, at home in Mulgrave.

In the wheelhouse, Leo Tarrant, 19, youngest member

of the crew, who was making his fifth trip in the trawler, held the ship on a steady, seaward course. Like others in the Pat, Leo liked it aboard this ship, the more so because his oldest brother, Walt, 26, the boatswain, was one of his shipmates. The brothers were from Burin, Nfld., where they had grown up to love the sea.

The elder Tarrant was in the galley getting a snack before coming on watch to join Leo and deck-hand Walter House. House was another Newfoundlander who hailed from Port au Prince but who was now living at Mulgrave with his wife and two small children.

Down below deck, Max Dodge, 38, the trawler's burly, capable first mate, and his father, deck-hand William Dodge, 68, veteran among the crew who was affectionately known to one and all as "Uncle Billy," were asleep in their bunks. There were five others asleep or resting in the crew's quarters. They were Second Engineer George Barnes, and deckhands William Walker, Sandy Hayward, Jim Dominic and Charlie Dominaux — all from Newfoundland except Walker, who came from Alder Point, Cape Breton. They had just spent eight hours on watch and had finished their spell of duty at 11 o'clock.

In the engine room, Chief Engineer John MacDonald kept the trawler at full speed ahead. There was still sufficient visibility to do this with safety. Like other married men in the crew, MacDonald hoped it would be a short trip so he could return to his wife and three children.

The remaining member of the crew and, by some standards, its most important was Jimmy Nickerson, 50, of Clark's Harbor, N.S., the Pat's lean, good-humored cook who had shipped with many of those aboard for 17 years. Despite the ribbing he took from his shipmates, Jimmy figured they were "the best gang I ever sailed with."

Nickerson was whipping up a noonday meal of fish and potatoes when, suddenly, a down draft caused an explosion in the oil stove before which he was standing. He was unable to leap back before a great flame shot into his face, searing the bridge of his nose and the whole front of his face. He managed to close his eyes in time to escape injury to them.

Walt Tarrant heard the explosion and looked up at the cook's cry of anguish. Tarrant leaped toward the stove to try to beat out the fire but within moments the entire galley was ablaze. Tarrant dashed for the galley exit, his bushy hair afire. Before he could extinguish it the fire had burned off all his hair and severely burned the top of his head.

Nickerson slammed the galley door shut in an effort to seal off the fire and smashed a finger of his left hand in his haste. In his excitement, he was hardly aware of the pain. The frightened cook dashed down the ladder to the engine room and yelled excitedly to Chief MacDonald, "Get out! Get out! The galley's on fire!"

The engine room was located at the foot of the galley and if the fire spread it would block access to and from that part of the ship. The engineer left the controls at full speed ahead and made his escape. Minutes later, the engine-room passageway was completely blocked by flames.

Meanwhile, Nickerson ran to the crew's quarters and aroused the seven men who were there. "Get out now, or you'll never get out!" he warned. "The ship's on fire!"

Max Dodge was one of the first out of his bunk. With all the fuel oil aboard, he well knew the hazards of fire. One of his first acts was to arouse his father. One by one, the men came up the ladder, past the burning galley. By this time the flames had eaten through the wooden galley door and it was almost impossible to get past. They barely managed to get clear before the exit to their quarters was sealed off. Deckhand Sandy Hayward, 35, a native of Fortune Bay, got clear by squeezing his body through a porthole.

An awesome sight greeted the men when they arrived on deck, some of them still struggling into their clothing. The ship's afterdeck was engulfed in flames which leaped high in the air. Great tongues of flame licked from the portholes of the galley, which was now an inferno. The blaze began to spread and the steel deck became red hot. The fire was being fed by an overflow of oil from the ship's stack.

Nickerson had also alerted Capt. Hillier soon after the fire began. The captain immediately sent out a distress signal over the ship's radio, "All ships in the area. Emergency. We're on fire and need help." But before he could give the exact position of his burning vessel, the radio went dead.

The captain's terse message touched off one of the biggest air-sea rescue searches in recent years but efforts were balked by the dense fog which hung over the coast until evening. By then the stricken trawler was many miles from the position where she had first sent out her distress signal.

While Capt. Hillier was getting off the distress signal, Max Dodge swiftly formed the crew into a bucket brigade and started dousing sea water on the fire. Because access to the engine room had been cut off, it was impossible to use the trawler's pumps to fight the mounting flames.

When the captain came on deck, he recognized the seriousness of the situation. "She's going to explode," he said, glancing nervously toward the fiery deck beneath which lay the aft fuel tank. "We'd better try to get the lifeboat off," he told Max.

As the skipper well knew, the lifeboat would have to be launched now or never. But what chance would there be to get it in the water without capsizing? The sea was rough and the trawler was travelling at full speed.

"We've got to take the chance," Capt. Hillier said. His idea, as confided to several members of the crew, was to put two men in the lifeboat — himself and Walt Tarrant. If and when they got the small craft into the water, the trawler was then to circle the lifeboat, close enough for the rest of the crew to leap overboard and swim to it. The lifeboat was big enough to hold the entire crew. It was a gamble Hillier figured had to be taken.

But there was probably too short a time for the captain to make his plan known to the crew before they scrambled into the boat.

In the midst of the efforts to get the lifeboat clear, Leo Tarrant saw his brother staggering dazedly about the deck, obviously in great pain from his seared and hairless head. Although the deck was blistering hot, Walt was barefoot and wore only a pair of dungarees and a T-shirt.

Leo started to peel off his heavy great coat to give to his brother. "Here, Walt," he said, "take my coat. You'll need it."

Walt looked at his brother for a moment before replying. Then he said, "Where I'm going I won't want it."

At that moment further conversation between the two ended when a heavy sea broke over the deck. The backwash carried Walter House overboard. Leo Tarrant managed to grab House's jacket before he submerged and with the help of Walt pulled him back aboard. House was a frightened man. "I can't swim a stroke," he confessed.

The pounding seas and the growing fire combined to frustrate the crew's efforts to get the lifeboat ready for launching. But after about 15 minutes, the craft had been lowered from its boom to the ship's rail. Nine men got in, including the Tarrant brothers. The others were Capt. Hillier, Chief Engineer John MacDonald, Second Engineer George Barnes, deckhands William Walker, Jim Dominic, Charlie Dominaux and Walter House.

But just before Max Dodge gave the "lower away" order, Leo Tarrant and Walker decided to take their chances aboard the trawler. They jumped back on the ship's deck. By then the deck was so hot beneath the lifeboat that Tarrant's boot stuck to it. In trying to yank his foot clear, he slipped on the deck, burning his leg and hands.

"Lower away!"

As Max Dodge gave the fateful command, all those aboard the trawler lent a hand. It was a tense moment for the men in the lifeboat and for those on deck. Was it possible to launch the craft in a sea like that?

The answer came quickly and tragically. The life-boat spanked down in the water and a great, rolling wave caught it broadside, turning the craft over on its side. Three of the occupants managed to hang on — Jim Dominic, Charlie Dominaux and Walter House. The others disappeared beneath the surface. The lifeboat was equipped with air tanks and rolled back into upright position. It was full of water but still afloat and the trio crawled back into it.

The little craft was still fastened to the trawler by the tackle used to lower it into the water. Max Dodge and Leo Tarrant cut it free with fire axes. It would have been too hazardous for the occupants to tow the boat at the ship's speed.

At this moment a new danger threatened the men aboard the trawler. The action of freeing the lifeboat tackle had released the ship's huge boom which began to swing crazily from side to side.

"Look out, Max!"

The warning came too late for Max Dodge. Before he could duck out of the way, the boom smashed into his face and bowled him backwards over the ship's rail. By a miracle, the burly fisherman managed to grab the edge of the deck and hang on. The trawler was low in the water and his legs dangled in the sea. By a superhuman effort he struggled back on board, blood flowing from a deep gash in his lip.

The injured mate's first thoughts were of the men in the water. "Take the wheel and we'll circle the lifeboat," he ordered Bill Walker.

The Sheila Patricia began to circle the lifeboat as those aboard the trawler kept a lookout. In the lifeboat one of the men was rowing and the two other occupants were bailing. There was no sign of the four who had been thrown from the boat when it capsized.

As the trawler circled the lifeboat, the men on deck

kept a close lookout for men in the water. They saw none. Max Dodge had hoped to get close enough to some of the swimming fishermen to throw them lifebelts. It was a forlorn hope.

The fire in the trawler's after deck still burned fiercely and was making the wheelhouse almost impossible for occupancy. Max tried the radio again. Reports were coming in but they could get nothing out. "Head for land," he commanded. At the wheel, Walker obeyed the order and steamed toward shore.

It was getting hotter in the wheelhouse and black clouds of smoke were seeping through. The choking fumes soon made it impossible to breathe and the heat was becoming unbearable. So Walker dogged the wheel (locked it in position) and escaped to the deck. He was gasping for breath.

From this point on the Sheila Patricia's crew had no control over either their ship's speed or her course. The fog had become so thick that visibility was reduced to a few hundred feet and scouting aircraft had to temporarily call off the hunt.

What if a ship or a shoal loomed up ahead?

The prospect sent cold chills through Max Dodge. He had a wife and five children at home. And, since the captain had gone, he held the responsibility for the remaining crew.

"I think we're going to be all gone," he whispered to his father and shipmate, Billy Dodge. Veteran aboard the trawler, Dodge, Sr., is a rugged mariner who has been sailing for 54 of his 68 years. The little Newfoundland-born fisherman had faced peril before. Once he and his nephew were adrift in a dory for 16 days, during which time they were without food and water. The nephew died during this ordeal. But Billy Dodge had enough strength in him to climb the Jacob's ladder of the Portugese vessel which rescued him. And on another occasion he survived when his ship sank on the Grand Banks.

"Nonsense, Max," he said. "We'll come out of this one."

Not many of the men aboard the burning trawler shared Uncle Billy's professed confidence at this moment. The fire was burning steadily and was beginning to reduce the superstructure to cinders.

"Look out. Here comes the mast!" someone yelled. The vessel's mast had burned through at its base and came crashing down on the deck. The crew had gathered on the forward deck where they kept pitching bucketfuls of water along the deck to keep the flames from spreading forward. None was endangered by the falling mast which carried the boom with it. But this wreckage hung over the port side and acted as a rudder which changed the trawler's direction. The Sheila Patricia's course became a zig-zag pattern until this obstacle could be cleared away.

Toward evening the weather began to clear and hopes grew that searching ships or aircraft would sight them. Great clouds of black smoke billowed from the blazing stern — a perfect signal for any searchers in the vicinity.

"I wonder when she'll blow," a deckhand said nervously.

That thought was in everyone's mind. None liked to think what would happen if the fuel tanks exploded.

Once, during a brief lull in the fire, several of the men made a dash for the refrigerator, back of the galley, and managed to salvage some food. They came back with grapefruit, eggs, cheese, oranges and biscuits, and one man found three bottles of beer in a locker. It was a risky venture but many of them had not eaten since early morning and were getting hungry. The food tasted good.

At 9 o'clock that night the trawler's engines stopped. The wind had died down and the sea was a heaving, dark mirror which glowed red when the fire flared.

Max Dodge had set the crew to work making a raft. If she blows, he thought, we'll have something to get away on. It was a crude, makeshift affair, made up of checker

14

boards (wooden bins used for dressing the fish) and floats salvaged from the trawls. The raft was lashed together with rope. In an emergency, they planned to heave it over the side and use it to buoy them up until help arrived.

A good part of the time the trawler's foredeck was awash and the fishermen's feet became numb with the cold. They had erected a stove on the foredeck and were feeding the fire with coils of rope. Leo Tarrant's feet were so numb he jabbed a fork into one of them and couldn't feel it.

From time to time the men would leave off work on the raft to swish buckets of water down the deck to keep the fire in check. The heat aft was unbearable.

Late that night the lookout spotted a vessel about eight to 10 miles away, apparently heading toward Newfoundland. Hopeful of rescue at last, the men started ripping off pieces of shirts and underwear. Max Dodge soaked these in fuel oil and carried them aloft into the rigging where he set them afire. But the ship continued on its voyage without seeing the trawler's signal.

Around 4 o'clock Thursday morning, one of the large fuel tanks exploded with a great hissing sound. All eyes turned nervously toward the afterdeck as the fire began to spread on the water.

"I figured we'd all be burned to death," Leo Tarrant recalled later. After the death of his brother, he said, he hadn't much cared what happened. But now he was prepared to fight to the last for his life. "If the flames attracted a rescue craft, I thought I might be able to leap overboard and swim to a point where the boat might pick us up."

But just about this time, Tarrant and his mates saw a welcome sight. A Dakota aircraft from the R. C. A. F. base at Torbay, Nfld., flew over them and, almost simultaneously, the coastal trawler Zebrula pulled close by.

Minutes later the Zebrula had put a lifeboat over and rowed to the side of the trawler where six weary survivors

15

piled in. Their terrible ordeal was ended. Soon after their arrival in port they learned that their three shipmates in the dory had died from exposure. Already Mulgrave has started a disaster fund for the families of the seven seamen who lost their lives.

2

CAPTAIN BUDGE

National Defence Photo

Capt. Budge, DSC, CD, RCN, one of Canada's most distinguished sailors, was promoted to Rear-Admiral and Chief of Naval Personnel at Naval Headquarters in June, 1960. He retired in 1962 after 42 years service.

The strains of O God Of Bethel floated through the salt air from an improvised chapel in the bridge structure of the Royal Canadian Navy cruiser H.M.C.S. Quebec at its Halifax Dockyard jetty.   Above the gently heaving

17

water of the harbor, a pair of inquisitive gulls hung in suspended flight as if eavesdropping.

A perspiring seaman, pausing momentarily in the task of polishing brass, said with a grin, "The Old Man's holding choir practice." Elsewhere in the 9,500-ton vessel, others of the 790-man crew prepared the ship for a southern cruise.

It was typical of 47-year-old Capt. Patrick David Budge, D.S.C., R.C.N., that with scores of pre-sailing chores to attend to, he still found time to conduct the ship's choir. Soon after his appointment last January as commanding officer of the Quebec, the music-loving skipper took charge of the choir.

Veteran sailors sometimes shudder at the unorthodox ways of this gray-haired, ruddy-faced officer who has become an almost legendary figure in Canadian naval circles. But, they all agree, he gets results. Pat Budge is a specialist at handling men. This happy knack led to his appointment as executive officer of H.M.C.S. Cornwallis when the "New Entry" training centre on the shores of Annapolis Basin was commissioned in 1949. And it was one of the main reasons for his appointment to the Quebec, which is primarily employed as a training ship for seamen. Budge is the first man in the Royal Canadian Navy to rise from boy seaman to captain.

Although he is a firm believer in discipline, he has never been known to punish an offender for violating a regulation the man didn't fully understand. "And," say shipmates, "he will never order a man to do something he wouldn't, or couldn't, do himself." His reputation for fairness is illustrated by the fact that he once stopped his own leave for arriving on duty a minute late. His talents range from being able to make a dress for his daughter, Wendy, 12, (which he did), to turning a cruiser on its heel in a confined space without the assistance of tugboats. Rear-Admiral R. E. S. Bidwell, O. B. E., flag officer, Atlantic Coast, who recently watched Budge put

18

the Quebec through this latter manoeuvre in the Narrows of Halifax harbor, classed it "a marvellous feat of seamanship."

The demonstrative type, he often poses as the horrible example at defaulters' sessions. While offenders looked on pop-eyed, he has been known to slouch, stagger, chew an imaginary wad of gum, swing his cap and tie askew and otherwise disarrange his immaculate dress, and lie flat on his back. He once ordered a seaman to kick him — all in the interests of hammering home his point that naval regulations make sense.

He is a teetotaller who drinks his soft drink out of a beer stein. In a foreign port, one of his first calls is to the nearest soda fountain to down huge quantities of ice cream.

The esteem in which he is held on both the upper and lower decks is akin to hero-worship. He is the only officer in the R.C.N. who was ever recognized in The Crowsnest, official organ of the lower deck, as its "Man of the Month."

His fellow-officers never cease to be amazed at his success in turning out choirs, for he can't read a note of music. On this summer afternoon, the voices of the Quebec's choir rose above the clatter of shipboard activity: "Our vows, our prayers, we now present before Thy throne of . . ." At this point, the music swerved several degrees to port and ground abruptly on a shoal of discord. In the chapel, Choirmaster Budge glared balefully at the semicircle of officers and men about him.

"Either Baker hit a wrong chord on the organ," he boomed, "or we went flat. And I don't think he hit a wrong chord. Now let's do it right this time. And I want every mother's son of you to put your flaming voices into it!"

The choir put their flaming voices into it. As the sun's heat penetrated the chapel, the captain peeled down to suspenders and shirt sleeves, scarcely missing a beat in the act. He thrust hymn books into the hands of a visiting reporter and photographer. In a Budge choir, everybody sings – or else.

Besides directing the ship's 30-voice Protestant choir, the Quebec's Anglican commanding officer frequently lends his voice at sessions of the ship's Roman Catholic choir. He has no patience with religious prejudice. Friends explain that it is not just coincidence that the Roman Catholic chapel which was erected close to his home at Cornwallis was named St. Patrick's.

Throughout his naval career, which began at the age of 16 when he ran away from home in Dover, England, and joined the boys' training ship Impregnable at Devonport, he has been trained to behave "in a seamanlike manner." This has become his creed and his favorite expression. The phrase is as much a part of his salty vocabulary as is the word "flaming." On Christmas Eve, 1950, the front lawn of his home at Cornwallis was decorated with a sign inscribed: "CEMANLYKE MANOR." It was put there by his commanding officer.

He is a stickler for proper dress. On one occasion when he reprimanded a trainee for wearing a soiled collar, the sailor said he had been unable to get to the laundry in time. Budge, then a commander, took the collar, washed it himself, and returned it spotlessly white. If there's one thing he abominates, it's a loose thread dangling from a row of ribbons. At a passing-out parade, officers and men concocted a plot which consisted of leading the end of a spool of thread from a chief petty officer's pocket to his row of ribbons. During the inspection, Budge passed down the line until he came to the C.P.O. "Very smart,": he said, "except for this Irish pennant." Whereupon he took the loose end and pulled – and pulled. As the thread unravelled by the yard he joined in the laughter which shook the ranks.

At Cornwallis, a trainee had charged an officer with kicking him – an unpardonable sin in the navy. Budge reprimanded the officer and imposed a stiff punishment. He suspected, however, that the "kick" had been nothing more than a nudge of the foot for slowness in obeying a command. The evidence showed that the officer had been standing close to the seated seaman at the time. When the officer had departed, Budge took a seat beside the standing tr̤ ˌee and told him to demonstrate exactly what had happened. "B-but, sir . . ." began the flustered complainant. "Go ahead. That's an order." The sailor kicked. Budge took the kick without wincing. "You see, I hardly felt it," he declared. But after he had dismissed the sailor, he gritted his teeth with pain.

A prized souvenir of his recent naval career is an eight-ball mounted on a mahogany base which today decorates the Quebec's wardroom. It was a gift from H.M.C.S. Cedarwood. The little wooden survey vessel recently pulled alongside the cruiser at Parry Sound, B.C., its loud hailers blaring out the swingy strains of The Thing. While the music played, the little craft's cargo derrick lifted a heavy, interesting-looking crate and set it down on the cruiser's deck. An officer pried off the lid, revealing bushels of sawdust which the wind whipped into a fog of flying chips. Beneath the sawdust were bottles, cans, pieces of wood, scraps of metal — and another box. Budge applied a crowbar and came upon more sawdust plus a six-inch projectile bearing a white "8". In still a third box, the grinning captain discovered the eight-ball and a plaque inscribed: "A Thing Not To Get Behind." The previous day the Quebec hadn't done so well at firing practice, and this was a reminder from the Cedarwood.

Ever since he was a boy, Budge wanted to go to sea. Although his father was a soldier, Budge was never partial to khaki. He says he hated his first year in the navy. "They used a rope's end pretty freely in those days," he recalls. "And I was homesick. But I didn't have the courage to quit." He is glad now that he stuck it out. His Royal Navy service included three years on the China

Station and a number of years in England. He transferred to the Royal Canadian Navy when his parents moved to Toronto in 1928.

His first command was the second H.M.C.S. Ottawa, which he took over in February, 1945. The following August he became captain of H.M.C.S. Gatineau, and when that vessel paid off at Esquimalt, Budge remained as first lieutenant of the naval barracks, H.M.C.S. Naden. The following year he was made assistant to the training commander there with the rank of lieutenant-commander. He later rose to training commander with the rank of acting commander. In August, 1947, he was appointed executive officer of H.M.C.S. Ontario. When Cornwallis opened, he was made executive officer of the base and after two years was promoted and given command of the Quebec.

His delight at being given command of the Quebec is understandable. She and her sister cruiser, H.M.C.S. Ontario, are formidable units of Canada's navy and pack a powerful punch. The Quebec carries nine six-inch guns, eight four-inch, and four three-pounders. In addition, she has eight 40-mm. and three 20-mm. anti-aircraft guns, plus six 21-inch torpedo tubes. Originally the Royal Navy ship Uganda, she was built by Vickers-Armstrong at Newcastle-on-Tyne and was commissioned on Dec. 17, 1942. The 555-foot vessel, which is credited with a speed of 31 knots, is heavily armoured. She was recommissioned early this year and renamed Quebec.

During his few spare moments, Budge loves to read sea stories, sing, and sew. Fancy needlework is one of his main hobbies and he has his own sewing machine. When he bought the machine he applied in person for the free course accompanying it. To his chagrin, he was turned down on the grounds that the course was "just for the ladies."

In his present command, as in all his others, Budge insists on the maintenance of high standards. On inspections, he has been known to wear white gloves and to rub his hands over all possible dust traps. If his gloves showed dirt at the end of the inspection, someone was hauled over the coals.

Those who know him have no doubts that, with Capt. Patrick David Budge at the helm, life aboard H.M.C.S. Quebec will be conducted ''in a seamanlike manner.''

3

TWO WHO SURVIVED

Three fishermen from Nova Scotia aboard the 42-foot longliner Maureen Rose set their lines in the North Atlantic fishing grounds, 35 miles southeast of Shelburne, and turned in for the night. Their vessel rode at anchor in a light swell.

At 5 o'clock next morning – Tuesday, October 19, 1965 – the men were awakened by a deep rumbling sound.

Harold Coffin, 30, the veteran of the trio, recognized the sound immediately. It came from the engines of a large ship. He leaped from his bunk and lunged toward the ship's radio to send an S O S.

He was too late.

Something exploded into the Maureen Rose and split it in two. Coffin caught a fleeting glimpse of a grey-hulled vessel with white superstructure before he went down in the cold moonlight sea. He came up spluttering but unhurt, his ears still ringing with the sound of the crash.

The Maureen Rose – what remained of it – was an awesome sight. More than half, including the cabin and lone dory, had been shorn away. Only part of the bow remained.

On its nose clung Cleverly "Clev" Smith, 25, who could not swim a stroke. Beneath his tousled hair his face was frozen in terror.

Somewhere beyond, the roving beam of a search-light stabbed into the sea. But the wrecked craft was far outside its arc.

"Help! I'm cut bad! Help!"

The cry came from Almon Smith, the Maureen Rose's 22-year-old, 200 pound skipper and Cleverly's brother. His right arm had been gashed in three places by some obstruction as he was flung through the cabin door into the water. He had swum to his ship's side and was clinging there in the blood-stained sea.

Cleverly edged toward the side of the deck to help his brother. First he assisted Coffin out of the water and the two pulled up Almon. Coffin ripped a piece from his own shirt and made a tourniquet to stop the flow of blood. It soon congealed in the cold air and the tourniquet was removed.

By now the exploring searchlight had vanished and the rumbling sound gone. All was quiet except for the lap of the sea against the hull and the men's heavy breathing. The lightly-clad trio sat precariously on the remnant of a boat and wondered what lay ahead. They were drenched and shivering.

In the pre-dawn glow they saw a welcome sight. A small fishing vessel was heading straight for them, a long distance away.

"It must be Claudie Brannen's boat," Cleverly said. Brannen was their neighbor in Port la Tour where all three lived. They began to wave and yell as Brannen's boat drew nearer. But suddenly, it changed course to haul trawl. Those aboard the other craft had neither seen nor heard them.

The sun came up.

"We'd be fishin' now" said Cleverly. "If only . . ." He felt a gust of wind and commented, "The wind's breezin' up to the north."

The wind began to whip up a sea and the waves broke over them steadily and relentlessly. At times the men went under water to their stomachs and often to their necks.

"I thought I was floatin' with nothin' beneath me," Coffin said. Before coming on this trip he had been first mate on a large marine-salvage ship. This meant long periods at sea when he never saw his family. So he had switched to fishing. And now this. Ashore were his wife and four children. Robin, seven, Richard, five, Patricia, three, and Brenda, two.

He and Cleverly began talking about their prospects of being rescued.

"Don't worry, boys. We'll be picked up," Almon interjected.

Silently, the wet, tired fishermen prayed it would be soon.

"Claudie's comin' again," Cleverly cried.

"He's not goin' to see us," said Harold Coffin. "If we only had something to reflect the sun."

They reached beneath the deck to look for a mirror that had been there. But it was gone. So they ripped away a piece of wood, tied a cloth to it and began waving and calling. Again the other fishing craft veered off and they were left alone.

Coffin's teeth chattered. "If we don't get warm soon we won't last long," he said.

As if in answer to his remark a blanket floated from beneath the bow and then another. He retrieved them and gave one to Almon, who was weak from loss of blood. He and Cleverly shared the other. At least it was some protection against the wind and sea.

They were still anchored and when one of the men suggested cutting it free, Almon objected. "We're better this way," he said.

The brothers thought of their parents and Cleverly prayed he would return to his wife and their children, Patricia Anne, 18 months, and Gerald, four months. Almon was unmarried.

None of the families ashore had cause for alarm,

being unaware of the Maureen Rose's plight.

As the day wore on Almon showed the stress of the ordeal more and more. If help did not arrive before dark, God help them all!

At 3 P.M. they thought their prayers were answered. They saw another boat five miles away and began waving their crude flag again. But no one saw them.

Almon was almost too weak and cold to care. So Coffin sat down and pulled him against his body to provide some protection against the choppy seas. For the next two hours the two friends stayed that way. In the twilight the sea became a cold, merciless grey and Almon's head fell forward.

Cleverly looked at his brother, his eyes reflecting his misery. "I think Almon's dead, Harold," he said. Both men knew it. Coffin looked at his watch, which was still running. It was 5:25 P.M.

After that they lashed Almon's body to the rail.

"There's nothing we can do for him now. We'll have to look after ourselves," Coffin said. The skin was gone from his right shin where it had scraped as the boat tilted back and forth. It looked raw and ugly.

The two huddled side by side, their heads together and two blankets about them to keep out the violent cold. They were half in the water.

"I've been cold before but never like this," Coffin said.

As the night closed about them the men prayed that help would come. But they held little hope.

They thought of food and water. Earlier they had found a piece of margarine and then a sea came and washed it from them. Coffin's mind was on three bottles of pop he had seen under the bow. If he tried to reach them he might have overturned the boat. It was too risky. Thirst nagged him.

Later that night they saw a ship's lights but again the vessel did not come close enough to see them in the dark. One thing in their favor; the wind and sea had died. But it was still very cold. Neither man had boots.

"If we get picked up at night it's goin' to be a lucky chance," Coffin mumbled.

Once they looked toward the spot where Almon's body had been tied, and it was gone.

"I'd hoped to bring Almon in," Cleverly said, his eyes tearstained. It was the first time they had fished together.

The two held council and decided to cut adrift and take their chances against the sea. Perhaps they might drift ashore. After several tries Cleverly managed to free the anchor and they began moving toward the coast.

Midnight came without indication of rescue. It was now 19 hours since they had been exposed to the wind and sea.

"I wonder how long we can last?" Cleverly asked.

The same question was in Coffin's mind. Neither knew the answer. They thought of their families and it helped distract them from their plight. Coffin kept thinking, too, of those bottles of pop. He felt like drinking a gallon.

Long after midnight, Coffin lifted their blanket to look out and he saw a pinpoint of light like the head of a match. Another frustration? But minutes later when he looked again the light spot was bigger.

Throats parched, the two began to call for help and the boat kept coming. At 4:15 A.M., Wednesday, Oct. 20, the fishing vessel Sheila And Kathy, commanded by Capt. Harley Dedrick pulled alongside.

After more than 23 hours at the mercy of the elements, the two men were helped aboard the rescue craft. The ordeal was over.

NURSE BENNETT OF THE OUTPORTS

Nurse Bennett with her merchant and seafaring husband, Angus.

"My toughest trip?"

The 75-year-old woman who is known all along the rugged Newfoundland coast from Corner Brook to St. Anthony simply as Nurse Bennett repeated the question she had just been asked, then thought for a moment.

Finally, after sorting through memories gathered as a nurse for more than 40 years in an area where until recently there were no roads, no doctors and no hospitals, she said: "I guess it would be the time Alex slipped under the saw and we had to get him to Bonne Bay, 60 miles away.''

That was in February, 1927, at Daniel's Harbour, and it began when a woodsman pounded on her door and yelled: ''Alex slipped under the saw! He's hurt awful.'' Alex was Nurse Bennett's brother-in-law.

The nurse and her husband dressed quickly, hitched up the horse and sled and, guided only by the light of a lantern, drove four miles into the woods to find the 25-year-old lumberman. He lay in the blood-soaked snow, conscious and in great pain. He had been pushing a piece of lumber into the circular saw and slipped into a pit beneath it. When he tried to climb out the whirling saw almost severed an ankle, through the joint. It was hanging by a slender strip of flesh.

Nurse Bennett applied a tourniquet, then had Alex placed on a mattress she had put in the sled before starting out. The trip back over the rough wood trail was torture.

As the sled jolted along all Nurse Bennett could think of was, ''Can he stand it?'' Late that night they finished the slow, awful journey and the patient was still alive.

''I may be able to save the foot,'' she told the patient, who was now lying on a cot. ''One artery is still there.'' The man was almost too weak to care. The nurse anesthetized the foot with snow and under the flickering light of a kerosene lamp removed loose bone and put the foot back in place. She bound it and made a splint of two pieces of board.

She sat with him all night and next morning telegraphed the nearest doctor — one had recently come to Bonne Bay — and asked him to come. She got this reply: ''CAN DO MORE FOR HIM HERE. SOUNDS LIKE AMPUTATION CASE.''

So at 10 that morning the nurse, her husband and the injured man travelled south, over ocean ice, since there

30

were no roads. Soon they realized it would be an ordeal.
The snow was deep beneath a light crust and with each
step the mare, Doll, went down to her haunches. After
several miles of this the poor animal was so tired they
thought it might die in its tracks.

"The   drift ice inshore would be firmer," Angus
Bennett said. So they moved inshore and for eight more
miles continued their journey, slithering and jerking over
huge ice pans which tilted crazily as they crossed.

But ashore, Mrs. William Isaac Payne, an alert tele-
graph operator at Parson's Pond, had heard of their plight
and began marshalling teams of helpers along the trail.

"I   don't think Doll will last much longer," said
Angus Bennett when they stopped for a rest. "Nor any of
us if this keeps up," his wife replied. All were dead
tired.

And then out from Parson's Pond came a group of
eight men carrying ropes. They were Mrs. Payne's volunteers. Never had the nurse or her husband seen such a
welcome sight. They had been on their feet all day because   the mare had all she could pull. Nurse Bennett
thanked God for the people of Newfoundland.

Quickly the men unhitched the horse, attached ropes
to the sled and pulled it over the ice. They were fresh
and pulled quickly but with great care for the patient.
They carried Alex Bennett up a 50-foot bank and pulled
the sleigh up after him. Others helped the weary nurse
and her husband.

Mrs. Payne had done more than organize help. She
had a fire burning in her living room and a large tureen of
hot soup. She found a bed for the patient, took one look
at Nurse Bennett and said, "Come, child, you go to sleep.
I'll watch." After some warm soup the nurse slept.

After an early breakfast next morning they continued
their journey over land. It was rough going in places and
often the horse floundered in heavy snow. But all along
people came to help, travelling with them a short way and

31

bringing hay for Doll. They asked about Alex Bennett and he managed a smile for them despite the pain.

All that day they pushed on in 20-degree weather. The nurse had made herself an aviator's cap and lined it with flannel and she wore heavy socks. Her face and feet were warm but she was terribly tired from walking beside the sled.

That night they reached Sally's Cove after a tortuous trip over the craggy hills around the coves. A group of fishermen and their wives came to greet them and the trio rested in the home of Mrs. Edna Roberts, who had baked for the occasion all day. The mare was given shelter, too.

"Poor Alex has had a rough time," Nurse Bennett told Mrs. Roberts. "I wonder how he can endure it." Mrs. Roberts was wondering the same thing about Nurse Bennett, who had walked most of the way, a 40-mile trip. She watched sympathetically as the nurse lay down on a couch and she removed her shoes as the courageous woman slept.

The third day of the awful journey began.

"We're getting there" said Angus. "It won't be much longer, Alex."

But it was longer than they thought. The road followed the coast and snowdrifts lay in their path. Skirting these was not always easy. But that night they had passed all the obstacles and moved into Woody Point, on the shore of Bonne Bay.

Here the area was more settled, and police gave their help. And the doctor arrived to examine Alex.

"He is going to be all right," the doctor finally said. "You've done the job so well there's nothing more I can do."

Today Alex is still alive, and still able to walk.

Mrs. Bennett first took up her career as a nurse to what were then some of Newfoundland's most isolated outports in May, 1921. Then she was Myra Grimsley, 31, a nurse and midwife who got her training as a district nurse in London during World War 1. After the war, still anxious to serve, she answered a plea made by Lady Harris, wife of Sir Charles Harris, then Governor of Newfoundland, for nurses. Newfoundland then was a self-govering Dominion.

She landed in Newfoundland at Daniel's Harbour in May, 1921, and the next day plunged into what was to be her life's work as the people of the outports came to her shyly and apologetically for help.

There were men with carbuncles, expectant mothers, some with injured limbs, and many with trivial complaints. Some came out of curiosity to watch the first nurse they had ever seen. Their teeth were very bad. The nurse had never pulled a tooth in her life but she pulled many that first month, without an anesthetic.

She had been there six weeks when word came that a woman in Cow Head, nearly 30 miles south, was gravely ill and not expected to live through the night. The coast had opened up and fishermen agreed to take her there despite a bad storm. It was a slow, dangerous trip but by 10 o'clock they reached Cow Head.

Her patient was a young woman who had just had a child without proper help. There was poison in her system and her pulse beat 160 to the minute. Quickly the nurse organized an army of helpers to stoke the fire and bring hot water. They worked all night and all next day. By midnight the next day the crisis was past and the nurse crawled into a kitchen corner and slept.

"Thank God you came," Rev. Thomas Greavett, the local clergyman said. "And thank God for them," the nurse replied, nodding toward her helpers.

News of the nurse's magic began to spread along the coast. Those who had been reluctant to come with their ailments began arriving from many points along the coast. The nurse, who worked for a $75 monthly salary, saw them all.

In 1922 she married Angus Bennett, a seafaring man

and merchant in Daniel's Harbour, and eventually raised a family of three children. She soon turned their home into a hospital. Often the two willingly gave up their beds so patients would have a place to sleep. She talked pregnant mothers into moving to Daniel's Harbour when their babies were due.

One winter evening she had gone to Bellburns to treat a patient and was about to return when a young woodsman sustained serious facial injuries while hauling wood. His horse had lashed out suddenly with its hoof and ripped away his lower jaw and upper teeth. He was in agony.

She drove him along the rough trail to her home, eight miles away, where she could treat him. When they arrived she bound his jaw with adhesive tape and for six weeks watched over him. When the first steamer came he sailed to Corner Brook where a doctor decided no further treatment was necessary. The man's jaw had set. When he returned the nurse pulled the broken teeth and he left gratefully.

Like the postman, Nurse Bennett travelled in all weather.

She loved dog-sledding. But on one maternity call to a village 12 miles away her dogs refused to go. It was too cold and windy and the snow was too deep. So she walked, stopping at homes along the way to warm her hands and feet. Wherever she stopped there was a pot of tea and some food on the table.

In one home a fisherman took off his boots. "Hey, Nurse," he offered. "Put these on." Her own boots were cold and damp and the fisherman's fitted, so she wore them on the rest of the journey. Sheer determination got her to her patient in time to bring a new child into the world.

One cold spring morning a fisherman arrived from Port Saunders by motorboat. "My wife is in labor and suffering. Will you come?" he asked. The nurse readily

34

agreed.

It would have been a five-hour sea trip, but a storm blew them ashore about six miles along the coast and they had to continue on foot. The trip was complicated by a year-old baby the nurse had promised to take to relatives in Port Saunders. Another woman had come along and all took turns carrying the baby.

The 15-mile journey was through woods and over barren lands. At Bellburns some teenaged children joined them to hold the child. At one point the baby's feet and legs became so cold the party entered a government camp and started a fire to warm them. They had travelled nearly 10 miles when the worried fisherman called, "There's a boat coming!"

Some fishermen had left Port Saunders and come through the storm for them. A short time later they reached their destination and the nurse successfully performed a difficult delivery — a baby girl.

Twenty-five years after she had started serving the outports, Nurse Bennett's work was recognized by those "outside." In the summer of 1946 Admiral Sir Humphrey T. Walwyn, Governor of Newfoundland, arrived at Port Saunders aboard an R.C.N. ship to give her the M.B.E. while her friends from all over the 225 miles of rugged coast she called her territory gathered to watch and cheer.

But an even greater event, as far as Nurse Bennett was concerned, took place two years later. At that time the Grenfell Mission opened a 13-bed station at Flower's Cove; Nurse Bennett and her people were no longer alone. For 27 years she had been almost the only hope these people — scattered over almost inaccessible terrain — had had for medical help. Now new facilities were becoming available. And things continued to improve.

Today, says Nurse Bennett, it is like a fairy tale.

"There are new hospitals at Bonne Bay, Port Saunders and St. Anthony, besides the Flower's Cove station," she said.

Recently a neighbor read that some people were returning their M.B.E.s because the Beatles had also been given the award. She mentioned it to the nurse.

"How silly of them," Nurse Bennett replied. "I'm not giving mine back. I earned it."

Nobody along the coast would argue about that.

AHOY, IT'S WILD ARCHIE!

Capt. Archie Publicover mounted this anti-aircraft gun on front lawn at LaHave, N.S., a relic of armed R.C.N. corvette he once bought.

Capt. Archibald S. Publicover is a fearless, wily, fun-loving adventurer whose nickname, "Wild Archie," has clung to him like a barnacle during a tempestuous, 63-year sailing career. Time and toil have lined his lean, ruddy features and silvered the once-fiery red mop which pokes from beneath his jaunty sea cap. But, otherwise, the years have taken no noticeable toil of this wiry little Bluenose skipper who is barely tall enough to spit through a porthole. At 71, he has muscles as solid as a ship's

37

anchor, he can climb a 100-foot mast as nimbly as a youngster, and he often puts in a 16-hour day as "admiral" of his four-vessel fleet at LaHave, N. S.

The flagship of this fleet is the sturdy motorship Maid of LaHave, which runs pulpwood from LaHave to New Haven, Conn. The others include a former minesweeper and a handsome monel-metal yacht. Capt Archie, a shrewd businessman, hopes to sell them both at a profit. The fourth vessel is the 50-foot motor sailer My Dream, which is sailboat, motorboat and lifeboat combined. Archie designed it himself in anticipation of a long pleasure voyage when he gets old enough to retire.

A fifth craft – a large-scale model of the former R.C.N. corvette Halifax – stands high and dry ashore on a platform in front of his home. Alongside it is an anti-aircraft gun. Capt. Archie says they symbolize his achievement as "the only man in existence who ever sailed the seas in command of his own private, fully-armed warship."

The Halifax was the first fighting ship sold by Canada after World War II. Capt Archie bought it from the War Assets Corp. in the summer of 1945 for $150,000. Through an error, the sale was completed before the vessel's armament was removed. By the time this oversight was discovered, Capt. Archie had his craft on the high seas, bound from Sydney to Liverpool, N.S., to have the craft converted into a freighter.

"I had a full naval crew aboard, as well as guns, asdic, depth-charge throwers and ammunition," Archie chuckled, his bright blue eyes twinkling. The incident created considerable consternation in official circles ashore, and when the corvette reached Liverpool the authorities tried to recover the armament. Capt. Archie, who believes that a man's ship is his castle, ordered all parties to keep their – hands off. He pointed out that he had purchased the corvette "as is, where is," and these magic words, he argued, entitled him to everything in her.

Capt. Archie later disposed of the armament and reduced his investment in the vessel. Most of it reportedly was purchased by the government. But he kept one piece, the anti-aircraft gun, which is the companion piece of the ship's model on his front lawn. The latter was a gift from the Liverpool plant which converted the corvette. About a year later, Capt. Archie sold the S. S. Halifax to Mexican interests but retained the model as a souvenir of one of his memorable voyages.

Some day, this hardy atom of the sea lanes plans to write his memoirs. They will probably include his own salty version of the Halifax incident. He will give a blow-by-blow report of his duel aboard a sinking three-master in World War I with a husky mutineer who was wanted for murder in the U. S. He will probably describe his encounter with another mutinous shipmate and relate how he subdued him with a home-made gun fashioned from a breech-loader and broom handle. An acquaintance of long standing often refers to Capt. Archie as "a 20th Century buccaneer," and his friends agree that this dough-ty little captain would have been more than a match for any swashbuckling pirate, had he lived in that era.

During his eventful career, "Wild Archie" has sur-vived storm, shipwreck, mutiny and countless rough-and-tumbles afloat and in sundry ports of the globe. He learn-ed to use his fists at an early age under the competent tutelage of the late Tom Foley, a Halifax boxing instructor, and he became handy with a revolver by shooting the necks off beer bottles in idle moments aboard his ship. The latter hobby was partly to sharpen up his shooting eye but primarily to show the crew who was boss. Shipmates said there was seldom any doubt about that. They declared the skipper could always be counted on to defend himself in skirmishes, whether the weapons were fists, broken bottles, brass knuckles, knives, or guns.

Without undue modesty, Capt. Archie himself says, "I've been through more in my lifetime than any other white man on earth." Along the Atlantic coast, where he has become a legendary figure among deep-sea sailing masters, this boast is not regarded as any great over-statement.

Capt. Archie is a man of many parts, none of which conforms to any recognizable pattern. When he launched the conversion of the Halifax, he didn't have a single drawing. "Anyone else would have had a stack of blue-prints," grinned the foreman of the Liverpool plant which converted the craft. "But not Archie. He had it all in his head. Pretty sound, too." Archie once designed and built his own coastal vessel without the aid of blueprints. Later, by the same rule-of-thumb methods, aided by a skilled Meteghan, N. S., shipbuilder, he produced a motor vessel which became a model for the Icelandic cargo fleet.

His varied roles have included that of salvage master, sea lawyer, general merchant, shipbuilder and designer and, above all, sailing master. Among his prized poss-essions is a handsome vase presented to him by the Japanese government for the rescue, during the early part of World War II, of 87 Japanese seamen. This marked the second time that a member of his family was honored by a foreign government. His elder brother, Capt. Andy, is the proud owner of a beautiful gold watch, a presentation from President Wilson, for the dramatic rescue of the master and crew of the U. S. schooner Henry R. Tilton in December, 1912.

Capt. Archie's nationality is something of a mystery. His father was a U. S. sea captain. His mother was Canadian. Archie himself claims dual citizenship in both countries and his lockers are filled with a variety of un-iforms to fit virtually any occasion. He was brought up at Dublin Shore, Lunenburg county, and from an early age was thrilled by the sight of windjammers sailing up the beautiful LaHave river. He quit school (Grade 2) when he was eight and began sailing in schooners under the hard-driving Bluenose "bully boy" mates of that period.

"Seamen led a tough life in those days," he recalls. "If you didn't 'Yes, Sir' and 'No, Sir' to the mate you'd likely get a marlinspike over the head. Or maybe you'd go overboard. I never sailed with my dad. He was a rough old guy and I was afraid he'd use the rope on me."

His first ship was the schooner Glendale in the Labrador fishery. At 13, he "went coasting" to the West Indies, was mate at 17, and became master of his own vessel, the schooner Acacia, at the age of 20. In those days only the hardiest wrestled their way to top authority. Archie says the Acacia's three "A's" have been good-luck symbols for him throughout his career.

He needed all his luck during one eventful passage in the early days of World War I. "I was master of the three-master William Thomas Moore and we had taken on a cargo of lumber at Halifax," Capt. Archie related. "Our destination was England. At Halifax I signed on a crew member named Scott who turned out to be a real trouble-maker." He described Scott as a husky, six-foot-three Negro. "Three days out of Halifax, the mate came to me and reported that Scott refused to work. I went along with the mate to get this fellow straightened away. I had a pair of handcuffs in one hand and a gun in the other. I wasn't going to stand for mutiny on my ship.

"Scott was standing on the after deck. Doing nothin'. He looked down at me and I guess he figured I was just a little runt. I told him he never got into the right ship but I'd try to make a man of him before the trip ended. I passed the 'cuffs to the mate and told him to put them on this fellow. At that, Scott started to call me a name and I shot him through the foot. While he was hoppin' around with the pain we got the 'cuffs on him and stowed him away in the cabin locker. After that a storm came up, and when we were off the Irish coast it got so bad we needed every hand — even Scott. So I let him out. That was a mistake. Scott grabbed a sheath knife and started for the mate. I grabbed my revolver and shot him through the hand

41

before he could do much damage. Then I ordered him up into the rigging and told him I'd finish him off if he gave us any more trouble.

"Things went from bad to worse that trip. Forty miles off the Irish coast we hit a German mine. Fortunately we had lumber aboard and we kept afloat for six days until help arrived. All this time we were lashed in the ship's rigging, Scott included. With a bullet through his foot and another through his hand, most of the sand was out of him. But he still had some fight left. When we were off the Azores after drifting in the storm, a rescue ship sighted us. But the sea was too rough for her to come alongside. Scott took a chance and jumped into the water. We all got off later the same way and were pulled aboard the rescue steamer. When we got there, there was no sign of Scott. I told the captain he was dangerous and we made a search of the ship. We found him hiding in the coal bunkers and the captain put him in irons. When we got into Fayal, the Portuguese police put him in jail there. I found out later he was wanted for murder in the United States. He was shipped back there, and that's the last I ever heard of him."

The audacious streak in Capt. Archie was well illustrated in the Nancy incident, which is vouched for by Eldred Bushen, of Dublin Shore, who was Capt. Archie's second mate at the time. The Nancy was a five-masted schooner which had been impounded in the port of Brest, France, on the orders of certain creditors, during a legal dispute over the repair bills against her. Capt. Archie was her master and had sailed to France with Bushen and First Mate George Sperry to sail the vessel home. But through the summer of 1924, while the wrangling went on, the Nancy lay immobile at her Brest dock. As a precautionary move, the wary creditors had removed the ship's engines and had placed a French watchman aboard. Furthermore, the government had ordered tug owners not to move the vessel.

Anxious to get home and aroused by the interminable delay, Capt. Archie decided to take matters into his own hands. While scouting about the Brest waterfront, he had discovered a government tug which had been idle for six months. He mustered a crew for this craft and commandeered it for one of the boldest ventures of his career. At 3 o'clock one afternoon, the Nancy slipped her lines, put her surprised watchman ashore, and, with Capt. Archie bellowing orders to all hands, left Brest under tow of the government's own tug.

"We kept looking back, expecting to see the Coast Guard coming after us, but I guess our departure took everyone by surprise," related Bushen. The lack of engines in the Nancy presented no big problem. In preparation for such an emergency, Capt. Archie had secreted aboard a set of canvas. Outside the port the vessel was favored by a friendly breeze and, after waving the tugboat crew a cheery goodbye, the resourceful skipper hoisted sails and made a successful, 52-day voyage across the Atlantic to LaHave.

One of Capt. Archie's lurid tales concerns a voyage in the schooner E. P. Theriault. "We had just sailed from Turk's Island with a load of salt," he recounted, "when I noticed that the crew were just sitting around. I asked one big fellow who was sitting down on the deck puffing a big cigar what the idea was, and he said, 'You'll do the work from now on.' I told him we'd see about that and I ran to my cabin to get my gun. But the crew had broken into my cabin and picked the lock of my closet. They had taken all my weapons."

Capt. Archie said he holed up in his cabin and worked out a plan of action to cope with the mutiny. In their haste, the crew had left behind a breech-loader and some revolver shells. The Theriault's master said he fashioned a barrel for the breech-loader by sawing off a broom handle and boring a hole in it with a brace and bit. He slipped a revolver cartridge into the bore of this crude gun and poked it through the cabin window.

"My gun didn't have any sights. I just pointed it in the general direction of this big fellow who was the ring-leader and fired. The first shot took him through the ear and he jumped up with a roar of surprise and pain. I told the others they'd get the same medicine if they didn't return the guns and go to work. I got my guns back and we didn't have any more trouble with that crew."

As a precaution against sailing with strange crews, Capt. Archie says he made a practice of rigging up an alarm system on the bottom step of his cabin. This consisted of a loud buzzer which would sound when anyone put a foot on the step. He says he often slept with a Colt in each hand and when the buzzer sounded he would be ready for action.

Sailing with Capt. Archie was an experience one former R.C.N. officer won't easily forget. This individual quit after several months' service under the Bluenose skipper. He explained that on several occasions, when the storm warnings were up and other craft were racing for the nearest port, Capt. Archie would keep his vessel on course if creditors in the port were hounding him during periods of temporary financial embarrassment.

Archie, who buys and sells ships as if they were cigars, has reportedly made and lost several fortunes. A shipmate who was with him in palmy days in Florida, says the Bluenose sailing master will be remembered in Miami as "a millionaire from Nova Scotia" who entertained his friends lavishly in a four-room hotel suite.

Although he is respected as tops among Atlantic skippers, he is among the most unorthodox. He frequently sails without charts and, in defiance of the superstition that it's bad luck to have a woman aboard, has often sailed with a woman mate. When he needs a ship and can't find one afloat to satisfy his demands and his purse, he may settle for a derelict. The schooner Maid of France, for instance, lay in the mud flats of Lunenburg harbor for several years until Capt. Archie bought her, salvaged her, refitted her. Similarly, he salvaged the freighter Clyde Valley from a reef off the Nova Scotia coast and made her seaworthy.

One of his sidelines is being a general merchant. Displayed in his store at LaHave is everything from a box of cereal to a grand piano. Several years ago he created a furore among other merchants along the coast by buying at jobbers' prices and selling far below the going retail price. When a rival store retaliated by publishing a "shopogram" alleging that Capt. Archie was giving his customers short weight, he saw red. So he mailed the offensive shopogram to the Halifax firm from which he had bought his scales. The firm sent a lawyer to the scene, but Archie and his competitors made peace before the affair reached the court. Archie's store is not a serious effort. He has left it untended for as long as three days without even bothering to lock the door.

This little mannerism doesn't surprise his customers, who recognize that Capt. Archie is not really a landlubber at heart. "Wild Archie" admits that the sea is still for him. He wants nothing more than a good sturdy boat, the open water and a stout breeze. If and when he retires, he will head My Dream to sea for a long, long cruise.

6

THEY BEAT HURRICANE BETSY

Capt. Harold Henneberry tells about the dramatic ordeal of the crew of the Angela B. Mills from the time their ship was wrecked by the Hurricane Betsy until they were rescued by a Newfoundland fishing craft.

Charlie Marryatt came into the pilot house of the Angela B. Mills on Friday morning, Aug. 17. He looked worried as he told me all the other fishing craft which had been with us had left.

I knew why he was nervous. The night before we'd heard a radio warning that Hurricane Betsy was coming up the New England coast. The other boats had apparently all decided to head in. We had talked it over and had decided to take a chance in the hope that the storm would pass between us and the shore. We were on the southwest corner of the Grand Banks, about 240 miles from the nearest land.

We talked it over again at breakfast and decided to go in. Charlie Burke, the Cape Bretoner in our crew, wasn't happy about that. He wanted to stay out and fish.

The weather was fine, the sea calm, and there was scarcely a cloud in the sky. Burke went aloft to look for fish and later the whole crew started to look. We had a tall spar 60 feet high with a cross-tree on which all the crew sits. From there you could see the fins of the swordfish cut the surface. As harpooner, I'd go out on the stand when we spotted a fish. We'd run the boat full speed until

I could strike it. Then one of the crew would get in the dory and pull on the harpoon line until the fish was dead. That sometimes takes as long as three hours. We stayed out there all that day and got 14 fish. We were so busy fishing that we made little headway toward shore.

We had begun running toward land again when we got a weather report. The hurricane was getting nearer. If we kept going we'd run into the middle of it. We decided to stop. We were all a bit jittery.

Next morning, Aug. 18, it was blowing a stiff breeze from the south. We pounded off to windward all day to make sure we'd be outside the hurricane.

About 11:30 that night, it was pouring rain and blowing about 25 miles an hour. The sea was growing quite rough, but nothing to endanger our boat — so I thought. I turned in with not a worry on my mind. I thought the weather would clear.

I had just gone to sleep when Charlie Marryatt dashed in and wakened me with a yell, "We're sinking!" Then I heard the other men running on deck and I knew we were in real trouble.

The boys got at the deck hand-pump while I tried to get at the pumps in the engine room. But the water was already half-way up the cyclinder of the engines, and we could only get one pump started.

I ran to the wheelhouse to try to call some boat or land station. The water was starting to cover the batteries, which would leave our phone dead. I kept repeating the message, "Calling any boat that can hear us. Angela B. Mills in sinking condition on end of the Grand Banks."

After 10 minutes, I knew nobody would hear us, as the lights were getting dim and the batteries were now under water. When everything went dark, I grabbed a flashlight and went outside , to find both pumps had become plugged with dirt from the bilge. The crew had three of our dories over the side. But the first one caught under the stern and we lost it, including all the food and water the

47

boys had got.

Roy Marryatt and I were the only two left aboard, so we tried to get the deck pump going. We got it working, but the water was still gaining fast. Then Charlie Burke came aboard and we went down to the engine room. Then I knew we had to leave our vessel, as the engine room was flooded.

There was nothing left to do now but to try to get a few supplies together for the dories. We went down to the forecastle. The sea water was now just three inches from the fresh-water taps. With Charlie Burke holding a flashlight I managed to get the teapot and tea kettles off the stove and fill them about three parts full of water. This water was about half salt, because the sea was rolling us about and splashing in salt water.

At this point a very bad thing happened. Charlie dropped his flashlight and we were left in pitch blackness. We went back on deck and tied the covers on our water kettles and I went back to the forecastle again to try to get some of the food. We had some canned goods in a locker under the stove but the water was up to my neck. I only managed to get a few cans. There was a door below leading into the hold and I pulled it open, but everything was under water. On the way up I managed to grab two loaves of bread and a carton of cigarets, as I knew the boys would need them. I don't smoke myself.

We got 11 quarts of whisky out of the wheelhouse, a handful of matches, an automatic pistol and bullets and a couple of blankets. We smashed two bottles of whisky throwing them into the dory. We were working against time. The Angela Mills was now listing badly and the sea was coming aboard. The rest of the boys were yelling at us, "Get off. Get off! She's going down!"

Charlie Burke had got back to his dory and there was one left on deck for Roy Marryatt and me. So I went and tore the compass out of the binnacle, grabbed the crank horn, and finally two old car tires which we used for fenders while lying at the wharf. We could use the tires to make a drag or sea anchor in case it blew too hard for us to row.

Roy yelled, "I can't get the dory launched – one of the tackles is gone!" It looked pretty bad. We both went to the bow and lifted it up on the rail. While Roy held it there I hoisted the stern with the tackle that was left. When she was high enough we gave the dory a push. She landed without taking in a drop of water, which was more luck than anything else. Then I grabbed a knife and we both jumped in the dory and cut the tackle clear. We tied a rope to the stern of the sinking vessel and then tied all three dories to this rope, one behind the other.

Melvin Gray looked at his watch. It was 3 A.M. – about two hours after we had first started to sink. We never did find out what caused that, although some of the boys recalled hearing a loud snap or crack when they were lying in their bunks.

Well, here we were, out in dories almost 250 miles from land. We had 23 cans of mixed canned goods, including juices, three small packages of sweet biscuits, about a gallon or so of water, which was half salt, our whisky and two slices of bread remaining from our two loaves.

After daylight the wind, which had been blowing from the southwest, hauled around to the north. It blew real hard and the sea became rough. So we untied the dories from the stern of the vessel and tied them to the centre, forming a lee.

Melvin Gray and Charlie Burke took a desperate chance. They went back aboard the vessel for a last look. Melvin got a sweater and my glasses out of a drawer and Charlie got a pint of rum. The oil was now running out of the fuel tanks and was making it calm around the boat. We cut the line fastening us to the sinking vessel and kept in her lee with the oars. Three swordfish went by and each came back for a second look as if they sensed something was wrong.

Toward sunset, we decided to head for land. Roy Marryatt and I were in one dory. Charlie Burke and Melvin Gray were in another and Keith Gray, Charlie and Herb Marryatt, brothers, were in the third. We had only one set of oars for each dory and I knew it would be bad if we lost even one. So we tied the oars to the boats. Then we could pull them back if they slipped from our grasp.

It wasn't long before the Angela Mills faded from sight. That's the last I ever saw of her. There was a lump in our throats, and maybe a tear or two. It was a blow financially, too — a $30,000 loss without a cent of insurance. But money was the least of our problems at the time.

We figured it would be about north to Cape Pine, Nfld. So we tried to keep a due north course. But it's hard to row a dory against the wind with only one pair of oars.

All through that first night we bucked a northerly wind, but next morning it changed to the southeast and helped us along. It was cold and rainy and foggy and sure uncomfortable. We were all soaked to the skin. The waves were so high we could hardly row.

"How long should it take us to row to shore if we're not picked up by some boat?" Keith asked me. I told him about five or six days. I thought it would take longer than that but I didn't want to worry him. Keith already had a lot on his mind. He kept thinking about his wife, who was going to have a baby. We found out later it was born while we were out there in the dories — a little girl.

Each man would row for a while and the others would try to rest and keep the dories bailed out. We were shipping lots of sea.

On Tuesday morning, Aug. 21, Charlie Marryatt rigged up a sail, using the blanket, a seat board and some of the fish gaffs. It was crude but it worked. We tied all the dories together and made some progress. Herb Marryatt's trench coat provided a second sail and we got along fine

50

that day. But toward night it began to get cold and we had to take down our makeshift sails to help keep us warm. A school of porpoise followed us for a few miles. We would have shot one of them but figured we'd see lots more. That was a mistake. One porpoise would have given us enough food for a week. We never saw another after that.

That night something went wrong with my eyes. I was seeing double. I'd gone without sleep for two nights and figured it might be fatigue. I took a couple of drinks of whisky and lay down in the stern. After a short nap I felt better.

Wednesday, Aug. 22: The wind hauled to the northwest and forced us to row too much to the eastward. The boys didn't like this and figured we'd never find land going like this. In the afternoon the fog started to clear and the sun peeked through. We took off our wet clothes to try to get dry, but an hour later it was raining again and we had to put them back on.

We got a scare at this point. A small whale had been following us for hours. He would come close in and roll his belly toward us. Two years ago, I recalled, a whale had knocked a dory fisherman 10 feet from the dory and smashed his boat — in these very waters. I kept thinking about that. After a time Roy splashed his oars at the whale and it left.

We tried to keep up our spirits by talking and doing little things like putting a chip of wood over the bow and timing it until it reached the stern. By this we judged we were travelling about 2 1/5 miles an hour.

"Our sons will never know what we look like," Roy said. I told him that our wives were young and that if we didn't make it to shore they could get married again. "That's a hell of a way to look at it," Roy replied.

That night Charlie Marryatt, who was in the lead dory, yelled, "I can see lights!" Sure enough, there were two boats. We nearly tore ourselves to pieces trying to get in front of them, blowing the horn and yelling. But we had nothing to make a light and they never saw us.

Thursday, Aug. 23: Today everyone was feeling pretty low about not being picked up the night before. We were hungry and thirsty and our food and water was getting low. We tried to catch some rain water, but it didn't rain hard enough.

The best I tasted was when Charlie Burke came alongside our dory and tossed in a can of pineapple, telling us it was our breakfast. It tasted better than any breakfast I have ever eaten.

We were getting so hungry that afternoon that we decided to try to shoot a sea bird. The first one I shot at I killed — so we had a little fresh meat.

That evening the wind swung around to the east and it blew so hard we couldn't even keep up the blanket for a sail. Then it became too stormy to even row. The sea broke in and filled the dories half full. The waves would whip the oars out of our hands and we'd have to pull them back in with the rope.

At this point we put out our drag (two tires on about 40 fathoms — 240 feet — of rope) and tied it to the stern of our dory. We put our stern to the wind and tied the other two dories to our bow. That night it blew 30 miles or more. Roy and I sat huddled with the blanket pulled down over the stern. We'd hear a large breaker coming and when we figured it was about to strike we'd throw up the blanket. This would ward off some of the water. We'd bail out the rest. We did this all night.

Friday, Aug. 24: This morning we started to row before daylight to keep warm. We'd had a bad night. Keith Gray thought of his wife back home at Sambro. "I guess the baby will be born by now," he said. "I wonder if I'll ever see it?"

Everyone said all the prayers they knew and Keith sang a hymn. Everyone felt a bit better when they got up and started to move. We were all so hungry now the boys were coaxing me to shoot another bird. I was so cold and shaky I couldn't do it. I shot at several and missed.

Later that day a shark about 25 feet long followed us but we chased it away with the oars. The boys wanted to shoot it but I thought if we crippled it we might be in worse trouble. It was big enough to bite off our dory's stern.

Everyone was losing hope of ever seeing land again. We thought of food a lot. Sometimes you'd speak to a fellow and he wouldn't answer. He was maybe praying, or thinking, or just too weak to answer.

Every once in a while one of the dories would draw alongside and one of the boys would ask, "Do you think we'll make it, Harold?" I'd tell them "Sure, we'll find the land if it doesn't blow too hard and sink our dories." This would rather encourage them and they'd keep on rowing. The whole crew was great, for what they had to put up with. Charlie Burke was so cold his voice was just a rasp. Charlie Marryatt had salt-water boils over his arms. Roy had a sore arm. The skin was all chafed off my legs from sitting on the dory seat. But we had to keep rowing.

About 8 in the morning we sighted a plane. He was only a couple of miles away but he didn't see us. Toward evening we were all feeling pretty tired and downhearted. The boys said, "We'll never make it, Harold." I hoped they were wrong. We had seen a gannet and one small gull, so I thought we might be getting close to land.

The wind had blown hard all day and we had a hard fight to keep the dories from getting swamped by the heavy seas. We could only take a taste of whisky now to make it last. But when one fellow started to talk about not ever making it, there was always someone to cheer him up. "We'll see land tomorrow," I told the boys. I wished I had believed it.

About 10 P.M. it started to rain so hard we couldn't row. So we put our tire drag out again. That rain solved our drinking problem. We knocked the head out of a swordfish keg and scooped it full. But the heavy rainstorm took the good out of all of us. I knew some couldn't stand another night like that.

At last the rain stopped. Some of the boys were feeling pretty bad. They lay down and wanted to stay. But we got them all sitting up and rowing for short spells.

I was going to nail my wallet and money to the side of the dory. It contained pictures of my wife and four children and about $2,000 in cash from the last trip. "Someone might get some good out of it," I told Roy.

Roy didn't like my plan. "Don't do it, Harold, because they'll all know you're giving up. Then we'll all be lost." I followed Roy's advice.

Saturday, Aug. 25: About 4 A.M. the sky cleared and the stars came out. We sighted a liner off on the horizon. We had nothing to signal with and she went by. As soon as dawn came I began to look to the north for a sight of land. I thought I saw it but wasn't sure. So I waited before telling the boys. Then when I was sure it was land I yelled, "It's land! It's land! Look!" But several of the crew just lay there and didn't even try to see. They thought it couldn't be so.

A few hours later we saw the sun on the great cliffs of Newfoundland. Everyone began to feel good. "We're going to make it," they said. We cut our dories apart and went single file. We started to drink our last can of milk and our last quart of whisky. It was 6 A.M.

At 2 P.M. we were still rowing and about three miles away. It looked as if the fog was going to shut down before we could make shore. We saw a fishing boat and started to row toward it. But soon the fishermen started to sail toward their harbor. I got the hand horn and blew a few blasts. Thank God they heard it. The boat turned around and headed toward us. Allan Sutten and his crew got us aboard their craft, poured some hot tea into us and gave us a meal.

We tumbled aboard their vessel exactly 7½ days from

the time we jumped into the dories on the Grand Banks. We figured we had rowed more than 300 miles. The fog shut down as thick as mud once again but now we didn't care. Our ordeal was over and we were going home.

Still alive and smiling after their arrival at Trepassey, Nfld., are the crew of a fishing boat that sank during Hurricane Betsy. The men rowed 300 miles through heaving, wind-swept seas. They are (L to R): Capt. Harold Henneberry, Roy and Charlie Marryatt, Melvin Gray, Herbert Marryatt, Keith Gray, Charlie Burke.

7

THE MAN THE SHARKS WOULDN'T EAT

Louis Jaques Photo

Veteran deep-sea mariner Capt. "Bertie" Himmelman, 86, breaks silence only now, 38 years later, after the mate's death.

I could smell trouble in the air the night before we sailed from Turks Islands, in the West Indies. It started over such a little incident. We had unloaded part of the Giant King's ballast before lying to for the night and some of the crew asked me if they could go ashore. I let them go.

As the men were leaving, the mate came up. I didn't like the look on his face. He was boiling mad about something. He was a big six-footer whose 190 pounds were all brawn and muscle. He came from a fine old Bluenose seafaring family. His name doesn't matter. I'll call him Mike.

When I asked him what was bothering him, he motioned toward the departing men. He said, "I'm mate on this vessel. They should have asked me if they could go ashore."

I told Mike he was making a lot out of nothing. But he wouldn't listen. He went off to his cabin, gathered up his clothes and headed for the crew's quarters. I figured he'd be all right after he slept on it, so I didn't bother him that night.

Early next morning I called the crew forward. Mike came up with them but he hung back and wouldn't take the mate's end of it. I ordered the crew to start unloading the rest of the ballast. Instead of tending the hatch, Mike went down into the hold and shovelled. I could see he was still in an ugly mood.

After we began to take on salt, he left and went aboard another vessel which lay near us. He was gone all day. That evening he returned and he had a good shot in him. I had planned to have it out with him when he came back but, in his condition, I figured it would have been useless.

We hoisted sail and headed for sea. Then I went below for the night. I hoped Mike was sleeping off his jag so I'd be able to get him straightened out in the morning. We carried a crew of seven including myself and we needed every hand.

Some hours after I turned in I heard a noise and woke up. I saw Mike standing in the doorway. He had a pint bottle of rum in his hand and he was pretty drunk. He lurched into my cabin. The cook, Eli Deal, came in behind him to see if everything was all right.

Mike said, "Let's all have a drink." He poured us both a shot. The cook gulped some of his but he couldn't stomach it. The rum had salt water in it. He spat it out. I managed to swallow a bit of mine and then got rid of the rest. It was awful stuff. Mike was furious. He glared at us and muttered something about Eli and I thinking we were too good to drink with him. I'd been pretty patient with him all along. Now I got mad.

I started to give him a tongue-lashing. I told him, "I've had enough trouble with you. Go lay yourself down and sleep it off. Don't act so foolish." At this, Mike swung around and started for the deck. He was beside himself with rage.

I hauled on my boots and went after him. He had a few minutes' head start. I was half-way up the steps when I heard the mainsail go. As the wind spilled out of the sail, the Giant King lost headway and veered off her course. It was dark on deck. There was no moon. Our vessel was pitching badly and there was a 10-knot wind.

In the faint light I spotted Mike on the aft end. He was running on the lee side and I caught the gleam of a sheath knife as he raised it to slash at anything that got in his way. If I didn't get to him fast, this rum-crazed mutineer would cut down all our sail. He was completely out of his mind and Lord knows what would happen if any of the crew was unlucky enough to get in his way.

I went around the other way to head him off. I caught him as he was making a sweep at the foresail. I swung at him and yelled, "Drop the knife, you fool!" The blow caught him on the wrist and the knife flew out of his grasp and clattered on the deck. He lost his balance and fell beside the rail. He lay there, half stunned.

"Get below and stay there," I ordered. I should have tied him up and put him below but we had to get our sails to rights. He started to get up. He was close to the rail.

I yelled a warning, "Look out, or you'll go overboard!" Just then the ship lurched violently, the mate lost his balance and went over the side with a scream of terror. Poor devil! I didn't give him much chance in that sea.

He was a strong swimmer, but even if he could keep afloat the sharks would probably get him before help arrived. I shuddered at the thought. The sharks were plentiful in these waters.

One of the crew, Ralph Joudrey, immediately volunteered to go after him. I wouldn't have ordered anyone to go. It was too dangerous. Ralph insisted that he'd like to make the try so we cut away the lashings from one of the lifeboats and managed to launch it in the rough water. Ralph disappeared in the direction where Mike had fallen overboard.

We had to leave them behind. The Giant King couldn't come around until we got on sail. We were now short two men. Maybe we'd never see either of them again. It seemed like hours before we got the damage repaired so we could turn back. I figured we had come about four miles from where we lost the mate, and we'd travelled a zig-zag course. The sea around us was black as death. It looked as if we'd never find our way back.

I steered myself and I prayed that I'd find the spot. After a spell I said, "I think we must be back." Then we lay to and looked out over the water but we couldn't see a thing. I blamed myself for letting Ralph go. I figured only a miracle would save the mate and it would be another miracle if we found Joudrey. That was too much to hope for.

The wind was whistling through the rigging and rustling our sails. Seamen have an old trick to blot out that sound. If you put your head down on the rail and listen you can hear noise that may be coming off the water. I laid my head on the rail and listened. Then I heard a faint voice somewhere off to starboard call, "Ahoy, there!" It was Ralph. By judgment and Providence we had found him.

Pretty soon we caught sight of the lifeboat and could make out the figures of not one, but two, men. It seemed incredible that Ralph had reached the mate before the sharks got him. I guess Mike was so bad, that the sharks wouldn't eat him.

We got the two men aboard and I told the cook to make something so the mate could vomit the salt water out of him.

The rest of the trip home was uneventful. The crew was jittery about Mike. We all kept an eye on him and we kept the rum away from him. Joudrey told us later that when he pulled him out of the sea and got him into the dory, Mike threatened to turn the boat over and plunge both of them into the water.

Shortly before we arrived in Lunenburg, Mike appealed to me to take him on my next trip. But I told him never again. We did one thing for him, though. We knew that if we talked about what had happened on this trip his career would be over. He was a good man when he was sober so we gave him a chance.

That's why we never told the story of the Giant King's voyage from Turks Islands. There's no point to keeping silent any longer. Drink finally killed him.

8

NIGHT OF TERROR

A survivor, Walter Williston (L), examines the remains of his boat to which he clung for four hours, until rescued by his distant relative Theodore Williston (R).

Tall, burly Theodore Williston, 28, of Hardwicke, N. B., who had fished out of Miramichi Bay since he was a little boy, entered the cabin of his 40-foot fishing boat Gulf Prowler and took a seat on the edge of a bunk. Tension showed in his weather-tanned face.

"Boys," he said to his two crew members, Aquila Manuel, 20, and Larry Martin, 24, both of Baie Ste. Anne, "if it weren't so late and we weren't so far out, do you know what I'd do?"

"No, Theodore. What?"

"I'd run for shore."

The younger fishermen looked surprised. Gulf Prowler had just made a three-hour run from the breakwater at Escuminac and was now 30 miles out in Northumberland

Strait. Her mackerel nets were set, her riding sail was up and she was ready to drift for the night. By morning she might well have a catch worth $75 or more — not the sort of haul a fisherman would pass up lightly.

Call it a premonition, or merely the sixth sense many fishermen seem to have when there's trouble ahead, but Williston was worried about the weather. When the three men left port at 6:05 this Friday night a thick fog hung over the bay, the sky was overcast and the sea fairly moderate. But now, shortly after 10 P.M., the northeast wind had stiffened and signs pointed to an unheralded storm.

None of the men in the 45 boats that put out this day liked the look of the weather very much. But foul weather had been the order of the week, and the official afternoon forecast pointed to nothing much worse than the previous four nights. Most of the fishermen readily gambled against the elements. For many of them, the gamble was to prove disastrous.

The first of the Gulf Prowler's series of mishaps hit around midnight when a driving rain, accompanied by rain, tore away her sail. Her crew tried to patch the damage but it broke loose again. The wind grew stronger and the sea rougher. The three men had crawled into their bunks after a late lunch but the pitching motion of their craft in the heaving waters made sleep virtually impossible.

By early Saturday morning the wind was blowing more than 45 miles per hour and the waves had increased in size. At 5 A.M. the little craft reeled under a sledge-hammer blow which catapulted Larry Martin out of his bunk to the cabin floor. He staggered to his feet, dazed, bruised, but otherwise unhurt. The blow was so severe that Williston thought his vessel might have broken loose from her nets and run aground. But a quick look outside showed they were still in deep water. Gulf Prowler had been clobbered by a heavy wave and had shipped a lot of water.

"We've got to haul in," Williston decided. As Martin and Manuel hauled in the nets, which contained a small catch, and stowed away the remnants of the sail, Williston got the motor started. He took a westerly course to clear the rockbound Escuminac Point, while his two companions began pumping out the water.

The sea was now a boiling cauldron. The combined action of wind and tide made the action of the waves unpredictable. Williston pinned a label on that sea. He called it "hateful." Gigantic waves seemed to build up out of nowhere. He took a firm hold on the wheel and kept his eyes glued to the tumbling seas. Drifting fog had cut visibility to several hundred yards and he wasn't sure where he was. Then, to make matters worse, Gulf Prowler's engine suddenly spluttered and died. After many anxious minutes, during which his craft lay side on to the heaving sea, Williston got his motor started again.

It was now nearing 9 o'clock Saturday morning. If Williston's calculations were right, they should be getting near the Escuminac breakwater. Thus far, Gulf Prowler had sighted only two other vessels that day, a passing steamer and later a boat owned by Roy Lloyd, of Escuminac, who was holding to his nets because he had decided it was too rough to haul in. Standing beside Lloyd was his 13-year-old son, Brian, who had gone along for the trip. Lloyd's boat appeared seaworthy, his engine was in order and he reported "No trouble."

But for Gulf Prowler, real trouble lay ahead. Williston had miscalculated his position and instead of approaching the safe haven of the Escuminac breakwater, he was heading toward a treacherous sand bar which is regarded as one of the worst hazards in Miramichi Bay. At five fathoms he saw breakers ahead and still figured it was the Escuminac shore. At two fathoms, he realized his error. He was almost on top of the sand bar. In a sea like that it would have been a certain death trap. Once aground on that deadly shoal, neither Gulf Prowler nor his crew would have stood a chance.

Just in time, Williston ran his craft back to six fathoms. A few minutes later he spotted the line spar which marks the salmon boundary north of the Escuminac breakwater. He now knew his position. He steered a northeast course which would carry him into deeper water when suddenly Aquila gave a shout of alarm, "There's three boats headed toward the bar!"

Williston gunned his engine and swung back to warn the craft of their danger. He recognized the boats as those of Bernie Jenkins, Placide MacIntyre and Jack Doucette, all of the Escuminac fishing fleet. The three vessels heeded the warning and headed away from the bar in Gulf Prowler's wake.

For Gulf Prowler, more trouble-shooting lay ahead. A short time later she came upon Raymond Thibeau's boat, which had suffered a severe battering and was drifting helplessly. It had broken clear of its mooring, its sail was gone and the engine was dead. It was in serious danger of capsizing in the raging seas. After a series of unsuccessful attempts, Gulf Prowler managed to get a line aboard the Thibeau craft and took it in tow.

At this point, Williston saw an incredible sight. Out of the corner of his eye he saw a great wall of water descending on Jack Doucette's boat – the 16-ton, 45-foot Francine D., one of the biggest vessels in the Escuminac fleet. "Jack's boat just seemed to ride up the side of this huge wave, which flipped it end over end," Williston recalled later. "It cleared the water by two or three feet, turned completely over, and fell – mouth down – into the sea. I have never seen anything like the power in that wave. It's an awful sight to see someone you know getting killed or drowned. I didn't think any of them would have a chance."

Miraculously, Jack Doucette survived this disaster and was able to give a first-hand account of what happened. From his post at the wheel of Francine D., the 43-year-old fisherman from Manuels saw the wave coming too late to avoid it. In 28 years of fishing he had never seen anything like it. It looked to him like a great big square wall with a foaming, 25-foot crest as it raced toward his vessel's bow.

"Watch out!" he yelled. "We've got it this time." The warning was intended for his two sons, Alphonse, 17, and Everett ("Evy"), 14, and for his close friend and neighbor, William George Manuel, 72, who had come along for the trip. Manuel was standing beside him and Alphonse and Evy were inside the cabin putting some gas in the tank.

The gigantic wave struck so suddenly that none had a chance to heed Jack Doucette's warning. "My boat flew completely out of the water. It was like being hit by a rock. I wouldn't have believed it possible," he recalled.

The two brothers were trapped inside the cabin when the boat came down. Their father came to the surface about 10 yards from where his boat was tossing, bottom up, in the surging waters. Jack Doucette had never swum a stroke in his life, but somehow he managed to reach his boat, which by now had turned right side up. He was half-drowned but by a herculean effort was able to crawl on to the Francine D.'s bow. The vessel was full of water but still afloat.

Glancing about him for some sign of the others, Jack Doucette was relieved to find that his sons were still alive. Somehow, they had managed to escape from the cabin. Alphonse was hanging onto the forward rail and Evy was swimming behind. Alphonse grabbed a mackerel crate and pushed it toward his brother, pulling him into the water-filled craft. William Manuel had apparently been killed outright when the boat over-turned. His body floated inside the boat and there was a deep gash in the head.

By this time, Bernie Jenkin's boat, nearest vessel to the Francine D. when it flipped over, was coming to the rescue. Alphonse recognized Bernie's nephew, Cyril, standing in the stern of the rescue boat. He had a coil of rope in his hand. Alphonse got in position to catch the lifeline. He and Cyril had practised rope-tossing and catching on the dock at Escuminac. They made a good team. In a sea like today's, manoeuvering close enough for Cyril to make the throw would require real seamanship.

On its first run, the vessel couldn't get in close enough for Cyril to throw the rope. Bernie Jenkins came around again in a great sweeping arc and this time got his boat within 25 feet of Doucette's. Alphonse caught the rope and quickly draped it over his young brother's shoulder's shoulder and under his arm. "Hang on tight. Bernie's going to pull you aboard," he said.

Evy obeyed his brother's instructions and a few minutes later was pulled to safety aboard the Jenkin's boat.

Alphonse looked anxiously toward his father, who had swallowed a great deal of water. "The next one's for you," he called. Alphonse wondered if his father would be strong enough to hold on to the rope long enough to be pulled to safety. He knew it would take the last ounce of his father's strength. He came to a decision. *If he loses the rope and doesn't make it, I don't want to go either.*

Again the rescue boat circled and came back. Alphonse got set for the most important catch of his life. Once more Cyril's toss was true to the mark. Alphonse caught the snaking line and passed it quickly to his father, who took a firm grip on the rope and stepped back into the sea. Somehow, Jack Doucette found the strength to hang on to the lifeline, and before long he was safe in the Jenkins's boat, where he fell face down, gasping and vomiting.

Alphonse breathed a grateful sigh of relief when he saw his father had been rescued. He was dismayed, however, to see the rescue boat head off into the distance. The thought flashed into his mind: *They're going to leave me here.* Gigantic waves periodically hid Jenkins's craft

from view. Apparently the huge seas were making it difficult for Bernie to turn. Alphonse figured the resce boat
had gone 500 yards away before he saw it begin to turn.
It seemed like an eternity to him before he again felt the
lifeline in his hands. Within a few minutes he was pulled
to safety.

"I wouldn't be afraid to bet that a third of the fishermen were lost in this storm," Jack Doucette remarked to
Bernie.

Fishermen who were lucky enough to reach shore
this Saturday bore out Doucette's estimate. They told
tragic tales of men washed overboard, of others
lashing themselves to the masts of their vessels, of sight-
ing wreckage which gave mute evidence of the disaster.

Within minutes after the dramatic rescue of the
Doucettes, Jenkins's boat was almost submerged by a
huge wave. Cyril Jenkins saw it coming and shouted,
"Look out, Bern!" But the warning was too late. The
force of the blow as the wave hit them broadside sent the
boat reeling over on its side and threw the engine off its
bed. The vessel almost capsized, but came back on an
even keel.

It was almost 6 o'clock that night before they got the
engine back in position and started again. In the mean-
time all hands had helped to bail and pump the boat comparatively dry. The weather was still bad and the seas
so rough that Bernie Jenkins and his companions decided
it would be safer to stay in deep water until daylight
Sunday.

When Bernie Jenkins turned back to go to the rescue
of the Doucette craft, those aboard Theodore Williston's
Gulf Prowler had watched from a distance. They could
see that Bernie was doing everything possible to achieve
the rescue. So Gulf Prowler left, still with the Thibeau
craft in tow. Eventually Thibeau got his engine started
and was able to proceed on his own.

Gulf Prowler had gone only a short distance when it

came upon the wreckage of fishing boats and equipment. Empty gas cans, crates, spars, bits of cabins, broken sails and tangled fishing gear all indicated the havoc the storm had wrought. Among the floating debris, Aquila Manuel saw a familiar sight. He recognized the top of a newly-varnished cabin and its black rail. "That's the top of William Chiasson's cabin. William's in trouble!" he exclaimed.

Aquila and William Chiasson were neighbors in Baie Ste. Anne. There was no mistaking the cabin. He had seen William varnish it. It was not until later that he learned that Chiasson, 47, and his two teenaged sons, Adrien and Robert, had been lost in the storm. William's brother, Albert Chiasson, and his son Alphonse, also of Baie Ste. Anne, were lost too. Albert's widow was left with 13 children, ranging from seven-month-old Charlene to 18-year-old Thaddee, who is in the Royal Canadian Navy.

A few minutes after spotting the wreckage, Aquila yelled excitedly, "There's a man back there standing up in the water!" Theodore Williston looked where Aquila was pointing but could see nothing. However, he headed back to investigate. Sure enough, there was a man clinging to the stern of a badly-battered, water-filled boat. As Gulf Prowler drew nearer, the man waved frantically.

Theodore recognized him as Walter Williston, 35, of Bay du Vin, a distant relative of his. Beside Williston in the boat was the body of a dead companion, Harold ("Hab") Taylor, 20, also of Bay du Vin. The pair had been in the water over four hours and Taylor had died from exposure. After two unsuccessful attempts to get a line aboard, Aquila managed the feat. Walter Williston took the line and tied it around his dead friend. "He goes first," he called. The rescue boat got Taylor's body aboard and headed back to get Walter.

Getting Walter Williston into the Gulf Prowler required all the strength Aquila and Larry Martin could muster. He weighed 200 pounds and exposure had so sapped his strength there was little he could do to help himself. His legs were blue-black from the cold and he had almost given up hope of ever being rescued. When they finally got him into their boat, the Gulf Prowler crew members carried him into the cabin, got his shoes off and wrapped him in a blanket. Gradually, the circulation came back into his limbs.

"Poor Hab Taylor," the rescued fisherman said later. "He knew he was going to die and he was worried about what would happen to his body. That's why I wanted to make sure he was taken off first. If they couldn't have taken us both, I wouldn't have left him."

Walter Williston, who has a wife and three children, has since become known as "the luckiest man in Bay du Vin." Fourteen of his companions from that tiny village never returned.

Among the rescued was Edward Cook, 28, of Howard's Cove, Prince Edward Island, who had been out fishing with his father, Fraser, 60, when the storm struck. The son lashed himself to the mast and advised his father to do the same. But Fraser Cook was trying to get the engine started and didn't take the advice. He was washed overboard before his son's eyes. Hours later Roy Lloyd's boat came along and rescued Edward.

Many of the stories of the disaster will remain untold. There are only bits of the wrecked vessels to indicate what happened.

As survivors straggled into port, the story of the tragedy slowly unfolded. They told of the havoc wrought by 75-m.p.h. winds and 50-foot waves. All day Saturday, wives and children waited anxiously on the docks. Some waited in vain. Others cried for joy when they recognized their loved ones. But there were many saddened homes. A grim total of 35 fishermen were listed as dead or missing in the worst fishing disaster the area had ever experienced.

The last vessel to return was Bernie Jenkins's. He

came in to the Escuminac breakwater at 7:30 Sunday morning, the Doucettes with him. "Other storms," said Bernie, "were just dolls compared to this one." The most devastating gale to hit New Brunswick's north shore in years, it had, as Jack Doucette had predicted, wiped out a third of the Miramichi fishing fleet.

9

ONLY FISHERMEN NEED APPLY

The island of Outer Baldonia is a three acre blot on the Atlantic seascape 12 miles off Wedgeport, N. S. It may be seen to best advantage through a dense fog. One of 300 islands in the Tusket group, this treeless mound of grass-topped gravel is inhabited by 50 sheep.

In any contest, to name the most romantic spot on earth, windswept, storm-lashed Outer Baldy would be a worthy rival of Lower Slobbovia for the booby prize.

A few months ago, Russell Arundel, a wealthy Washington, DC, big game sportsman, approached the group of Wedgeport tuna and lobster fishermen who owned Outer Baldy and startled them by announcing: "I'd like to buy your island." Before the owners had recovered from their surprise, Arundel put $750 on the line and Outer Baldy was his.

"Why," asked a mystified Wedgeport villager, "would anyone pay real money for a place like that? I'd look twice at a nickel before I'd swap it for Baldy."

Arundel swiftly cleared up this mystery. He proposed, he said, to set up the Principality of Outer Baldonia on his pint-sized island. Basically it would outlaw taxes, inhibitions, double talk and women. The new principality would recognize the laws of Nova Scotia but would have certain ironbound laws of its own.

These were set out by "Prince of Princes" Arundel

in a Declaration of Independence. He also announced that official seals, stamps, flags, passports, and legal forms were being prepared in London.

Outer Baldonia's Declaration of Independence reads: "Let these facts be submitted to a candid world:

"That fishermen are a race alone. That fishermen are endowed with the following inalienable rights: The right to lie and be believed. The right of freedom from question, nagging, shaving, interruption, women, taxes, politics, war, monologues, cant and inhibitions. The right to applause, vanity, flattery, praise and self-inflation. The right to swear, lie, drink, gamble and silence. The right to be noisy, boisterous, quiet, pensive, expansive and hilarious. The right to choose company and the right to be alone. The right to sleep all day and stay up all night.

"KNOW YE! That these rights, being inalienable and self-evident and contrary to social customs of the world, make fishermen a race separate and apart from all other races . . ."

Although some of his contemporary rulers would be perfectly happy if all of their subjects were sheep, Prince Arundel wanted citizenry of the highest intelligence, namely men. He welcomed to the principality all red-blooded males who had proved their vitality by fighting or boating a tuna. Each of the Wedgeport guides would be an admiral and each member a prince. Provided they are acceptable to the newly-formed International Tuna Club, designated as the owner of the principality, and qualify under the rules, outsiders can join on payment of anything from $50 to $100. Membership is limited to 100 persons.

Arundel soon cleared up speculation about the future of the sheep. "Your Prince," he pronounced, "has granted to certain of his Liegemen the right to graze sheep on the uplands of Outer Baldonia for the remainder of their natural lives. But," he added, "we do not wish these creatures

to become too familiar with the visiting Princes, or such
action might well disturb the utter peace and tranquility
of Baldonia.''

Housing and monetary problems were among the first
considerations of Prince Arundel for his principality.

He solved the first by commissioning the Wedgeport
guides to build a 20-by-30-foot beachstone ''castle'' atop
the island. In one wall of this $3,000 structure, which the
guides completed this year, is a huge eight-foot square
window overlooking the famous Soldier's Rip, a mere 75
yards away. The Rip is the scene of the annual International Tuna Tournament where sports fishermen from
many parts of the world catch giant bluefins with rod and
line. According to Kip Farrington, tourney official and
noted big game fisherman, it's ''the greatest fishing hole
in the world.'' Through this big window the Outer Baldon-
ians may derive a vicarious thrill from the fight to land
700-and-800-pound bluefins between sips of their Baldonia
Bombshells (rum with a rum base).

Over this temporary capital will be flown the Royal
Banner of Outer Baldonia — a blue tuna in white circular
crest set in a sea-green field. ''Our flags,'' reported
Prince Arundel to Ronald Wallace, of Halifax, his ambass-
ador extraordinary and plenipotentiary to Canada ''have
been authenticated and the first has flown over our Legat-
ion in the United States.''

In the midst of wrestling with Outer Baldonia's monetary situation, the Prince was mildly critical of Britain's
action in devaluating the pound. ''Your government was
not consulted,'' he wrote his plenipotentiary. ''Obviously,
our consent was taken for granted by Sir Stafford Cripps
because of the fact that we recognize no currency other
than our own. The Outer Baldonia tunar is the most valuable money in the world, because it can never be redeem-
ed for taxes — this odious practice having been forever
out-lawed on our beloved island.''

Recently, rumors of pending civil war on Outer Bald-

73

onia have sprung from the suggestion of Elson Boudreau, (secretary manager of the Wedgeport Tuna Guides Association) the bald-headed island's chancellor and "lord guide," that the "no women" law be repealed.

"I think we should let them join" said Boudreau in announcing the proposed amendment to the charter. "We get quite a lot of them down here tuna fishing and they may not like being kept out."

Prince Arundel moved quickly to snuff out this spark of rebellion. "I would say that visas for that sex must be the sole and dire responsibility of a Prince of the Realm, who, of course, must know that all other Princes are bound by oath to shed their inhibitions when they step ashore. Who, then, would risk his fair companions under such circumstances?"

Should war, or the threat of war, come to Outer Baldonia's shores, Prince Arundel stands ready to stamp it out. His Canadian plenipotentiary is an official of the Armdale Yacht Club, of Halifax, whose 101 ships and 400 men form a powerful wing of the Outer Baldonian Navy.

Unlike its neighbors, Mossy Bald, Half Bald, and Inner Bald, the Island of Outer Baldonia refuses to recognize the Gregorian calendar. Its rulers have substituted OB for AD, so that on the Baldonian calender the present year is OB 1.

The island's seven-man Board of Governors warns that transposition of these letters is an offence against the realm. "BO," announced an official spokesman, "is something else entirely." This error may well have originated from the perfume emanating from Outer Baldonia's sheep, which bears no similarity to the bottled variety on the cosmetic counters.

10

NIGHTMARE THAT CAME TRUE

After ordeal in the North Atlantic, shipmates Robert Mayo (L) and Bernie Mosher stand along port rail of Lunenburg dragger Cape Eagle.

Lean, tall Bernie Mosher, 17, was picking scallops from the foredeck of the Lunenburg dragger Cape Eagle during a North Atlantic gale when the big wave struck.

Before the youth had a chance to look up, a curling wall of green, foam-crested water raced toward him, snatched him from the canted deck, and flung him over the starboard rail. His scream for help was choked off by the howl of a 33-knot wind, and he struggled to the surface of the tossing ocean just in time to see the Cape Eagle's stern go by at a seven-knot clip.

The fear that none of his shipmates was aware of his plight chilled Mosher more than the icy seas. The rest of the 20-man crew had been aft. The waves and flying spray would have blotted out their view of the foredeck.

He knew his life hung on a quick rescue. Already he could feel the numbing cold of the seas through his heavy rubber boots and oilskin jacket. It was now 1:30 o'clock on a cold February afternoon, 1962. The place: George's Bank, about 200 miles south of Yarmouth, N. S.

As Mosher watched, he saw a heartening sight. The dragger began to circle back toward him.

Unlike many fishermen, he was a strong swimmer. He struck out slowly toward the vessel. But he died a little when the Eagle's first run was wide.

"I can't hold out much longer!" Mosher yelled as the dragger washed by. Through a blur he could see his shipmates by the rail. He knew that among them would be his lifelong friend and neighbor, Bob Mayo.

The dragger changed direction and began to come back stern-first. Mosher heard voices above the noise of the wind and waves. Suddenly a ship's life ring was less than a foot from him. His brain told him to reach for it, but his numb, leaden arms would not respond.

A big wave struck him and he was under water again, in a happy, blissful, unconscious world. Another wave flung him to the surface, face up, reviving him.

He saw the shadow of the dark-hulled Cape Eagle less than a ship's length away and the flash of a white body plunging into the sea. Instinct told him it was Bob Mayo, then he lost consciousness and began to sink.

Mayo had awaited his chance. For five minutes before the opportunity came he stood naked at the ship's rail. He was bitterly cold but unaware of it. His determination to save Mosher was so deep-rooted he defied the elements.

Vividly Mayo recalled an incident three months earlier. Bernie had come over to see him full of a nightmare he had had the night before. "In my dream I saw myself being washed overboard. You saved my life," he told Mayo. They both laughed and forgot about it.

As Mayo plunged naked into the Atlantic and struck out toward his chum, he prayed everything would work out the way it had in the dream. He was no stranger to the perils of the sea. In the winter of 1961, Mayo and his father had jumped into the sea to help free two fishermen trapped in a fouled net.

He had helped save those lives, but now, just as he completed the 50-yard swim, Bernie Mosher was slipping unconscious beneath the surface again. Mayo duck-dived after him and hauled him to the surface by the hair.

"It was the happiest time of my life when I got my hands on Bernie," Mayo says.

The swim back was a superhuman effort. Three times waves broke Mayo's hold and Mosher started to go down. On each occasion Mayo dragged him back.

Although near exhaustion when the crew pulled them over the side of the Cape Eagle, Mayo stayed to give artificial respiration. Only when Mosher showed signs of life did he go below. Then he stumbled down the companionway, wrapped himself in a blanket and sat shivering by the stove for two solid hours.

Within 12 hours of the ordeal both men were back at work in the shucking house, shelling scallops. Suddenly Mayo bellowed at Mosher, "What's the idea of swiping my scallops?" He accompanied the query with a well-directed boot that sent Mosher flying.

Mosher came back swinging at his buddy and connected with a haymaker to the chin. In seconds, the life-saver and the survivor were brawling on the deck.

At this point crewmates moved in and separated them. Within minutes, the belligerent pair were grinning and shucking again. When the Cape Eagle docked they headed home side by side, talking not of the sea, but of a planned trip to Mexico when they got the money.

But, though Mayo sailed on the Cape Eagle's next trip five days later, Mosher picked another dragger. "I'm not superstitious," he said. "I think I need a change."

11

TWO DIED JUST 50 YARDS FROM SHORE

Lookouts Hector Williams, 42, a nimble five-footer whose 146 pounds are all bone, sinew and muscle, and his burly shipmate Rayburn Zinck, 43, clung to the pitching bow of the fishing boat, Ray-Ola-K as it plowed through a nor'east blizzard one recent winter evening toward its home port of Shelburne, N.S. Too late — a few yards off the port bow — they saw the menacing breakers and yelled a warning.

Capt. Joe Enslow, a seasoned veteran of 47 who had sailed safely through many a storm, swung the wheel hard over but his boat had no time to come around. She grounded with a crash on the sharp rocks of MacNutt's Island, as deadly a trap as exists along this stretch of the Atlantic seaboard. The 59-foot two-master held hard and fast on a shoal which mariners know, without affection, as "The Sisters." The waves, boiled up by a 40-mile-an-hour wind, began to pound the boat to pieces.

At the moment of the crash — about 6:30 P.M. — Ray-Ola-K got away a distress signal which started an air-sea rescue search. But the search was hampered by the storm, which reduced visibility to near zero. And soon after the grounding, the radio went dead.

The Ray-Ola-K had left Shelburne a few days earlier with a crew of five. She had her catch and was almost home when she missed the harbor mouth and struck the nearby shoal. She had no radar.

"Get the dory out!" Capt. Enslow ordered.   He figured there might be a chance for the crew to reach shore
in the ship's lone lifeboat.   But launching it was easier
said than done.   The men tried to put it over the aft end
but found the way blocked by two huge rocks lying just
beneath the vessel's stern.   Then they started to heave
and wrestle it across the hatch to put it in the sea on the
port side.

It was dangerous and laborious work which required
all hands.   At times the swirling snow blotted out vision
completely.   And there was always the danger of being
washed overboard by a wave.

Eventually the crew got the dory over the side and
Ray Zinck climbed down into it to bail out some of the
water when suddenly a wave pitched the dory in the air.
The motion caught Zinck off balance and plunged him into
the sea, between the dory and the Ray-Ola-K.

A powerful man, Zinck had been in tight spots before.
Once while fishing off the St. Pierre banks he had saved
his   own   life and that of his father when his dory was
swamped by a heavy sea.   On another occasion he had held
on until help came after falling through the ice while seal-
ing in the Strait of Belle Isle.   This time he managed to
grab Ray-Ola-K's side and Capt. Enslow reached down
and pulled him aboard.

The crew was still trying to abandon the doomed vessel when someone called out, "Luke's in the water!"   A
sudden wave had struck Luke Berringer, 48, the oldest
member of the crew, and flung him into the sea.

Capt. Enslow heard Luke's scream, dashed to the ship's
rail and, as Luke came to the surface, he leaned over and
grabbed his outstretched hand.   Ray Zinck and Hec Williams
started to lend a hand.   Just then Hec looked back over his
shoulder and saw a great mountain of water about to hit the
Ray-Ola K broadside.

"There's a big sea comin'!" he yelled.

John "Sonny" Guy, 28, a six-foot, 178 pound husky,

the youngest man in the crew, was at the Ray-Ola-K's rail with a tight hold on the dory. He looked toward where Hec was pointing and tensed himself for the blow.

The courageous skipper never once looked up. Nor did he relax his grip on Luke Berringer's hand. He was too busy trying to save a shipmate's life to think of his own safety. His valor cost him his life.

The wave crashed down on the helpless vessel and its trapped occupants like a giant sledge-hammer.

"The sound of that wall of water," said Sonny Guy later, "was worse than thunder — just crashing all the time."

When the sea receded, there were only three men left on deck. Sonny Guy, Ray Zinck and Hec Williams rubbed the water out of their eyes and staggered to their feet. They stared in disblief at the spot where Joe Enslow had been bending over holding on to Luke Berringer. They looked around for the dory. All had vanished.

Hec Williams, stunned and bewildered, kept staring at the spot where his two shipmates had been moments earlier. "Joe and Luke's gone," he mumbled. "They're gone."

But the storm continued without letup. Ray-Ola-K was now virtually in two pieces. The only thing holding her together was her driveshaft. The afterdeck was such a shambles that the three survivors figured their only chance would be to remain on the foredeck, where the wheelhouse would provide a little shelter and the rigging would give them something to grasp.

Williams, who could not swim, wanted to stay with the boat to the last, rather than try to reach shore, about 50 yards away. His shipmates, too, knew the danger of an attempt to reach land. A man could easily be dashed to death in the tangle of surf-lashed rocks or die from exposure in the icy seas should he try to wade or swim ashore.

Hec Williams was making his way forward when a

80

sudden wave caught him and drove him against a door of the wheelhouse. He winced with pain from a broken rib, but kept on.

The men decided the safest spot was on the leeward side of the wheelhouse. "We're not hurt and we're still breathin'," Hec Williams said. "We've got somethin' to hang on to. We might as well hang on as long as we can. Maybe she'll float when the tide comes back. If that happens, the wind will drive her in closer to shore and we may have a better chance."

It seemed like a forlorn hope. But it was a hope.

About two hours after the boat grounded, the men saw lights to seaward and knew the search for them had begun. They learned later that Capt. Ivan Scott, of the Terry And Gail, Capt. Keith Williams, of the Blue Swan, and Capt. Gerald Hemeon, with his lobster boat, were hunting for them.

Ray Zinck had taken a firm hold in between the wheelhouse and the rigging and had a tight grip on Sonny Guy, who was in a less secure spot. At first the wheelhouse gave the three some protection, but the weight of the sea and wind broke down its door and before long the foredeck was littered with debris. Time and again, a sea would whip through the remnants of the wheelhouse and take Sonny Guy out over the side. Each time Ray Zinck would pull him back to safety. "He saved my life many times," says Guy today.

When the tide came back, Ray-Ola-K showed no sign of budging. It was now around 11 P.M. The boat had been on the shoal about 4½ hours and had taken a terrible beating. There wasn't much left of her.

Suddenly a big sea broke her stern, which swung the bow in closer toward shore.

Ray Zinck nudged Sonny Guy and said: "Now we might make it, Sonny."

Guy made a leap from the deck for a big rock, missed his footing and disappeared beneath the surface between the Ray-Ola-K and the rock. He was wearing his oil-skins and his hip boots and they weighed him down. But he came up and managed to crawl clear just as the bow crashed against the rock. Somehow – it is all now just a vague, unpleasant memory – he managed to wade, stagger, and stumble through the freezing waters to the beach, where he collapsed.

Hec Williams and Ray Zinck, who came behind, found Sonny lying there. "My legs are paralyzed," he told them. "I can't walk." All three men were wet and cold and weary from wading ashore. MacNutt's Island is three miles long, and uninhabited, but there is a lighthouse at the far end. Hec and Ray helped their younger shipmate to his feet and, somehow, they climbed a short, rocky incline to a fir grove. Here, they made a shelter for the night.

First they sat down, pulled off each other's boots and drained the water from them. Then they took off their socks and tried to wring out the water. They twisted their socks furiously until their hands became so cold they could do it no longer. Then they got up and beat their arms and danced around to try to keep warm.

Sonny's legs were in bad shape. He was so unbearably weary he lay down and started to go to sleep. Ray and Hec shook him. "If you go to sleep you'll freeze to death," they told him.

The young fisherman got to his feet and started to move around as well as he could, numb with the cold. It was now the early hours of the morning and the wind seemed to be dying down a bit. But the cold was still intense.

Guy, the most lightly-clad of the three, wondered if he could last the night. He thought how nice it would be to be home with his mother and father. He began to pray silently. "I told the Lord," he said later, "that if He got me out of this scrape I'd mend my ways. I didn't think we had much chance. I don't think Rayburn thought so either."

The others, too, were thinking of their loved ones – Ray Zinck has an eight-year-old daughter Linda, and Hec

Williams four children, aged one to 10. They wondered if they would ever see their homes again. The thought gave them the energy to fight on.

Somehow they survived the night. At dawn they straggled down to the shore. There, Capt. Scott and the crew of the Terry And Gail spotted them and their ordeal was over.

12

LIVEST GHOST AFLOAT

Captain Haycock

Carleton Augustus Winchester Haycock, 53, a battle-scarred veteran of two world wars, is probably the livest ghost afloat.

Believed by his family to have been killed in action at Passchendaele in October, 1917, the rugged, 200-pound Nova Scotian turned up safe and moderately sound recently as fourth engineer in the tanker Imperial Toronto.

During the 35 years since his "death," Haycock lived an adventurous life. In sundry mishaps ashore and afloat, the personable gray-haired seaman sustained such assorted injuries as bullet-riddled legs, a smashed foot, a broken arm, severe frostbite, a dislocated shoulder,

84

numerous broken ribs, a variety of body bruises, and a broken neck which he will likely have for the rest of his days because of the danger of an operation.

A shipmate, noting Haycock's love of cats, once observed dryly, "It's understandable. They both have nine lives."

Recently, a half-brother, Archie Hayward, of Jonesport, Me., arrived in Westport, N. S., to look for Haycock's grave. When he asked the village storekeeper to direct him to the cemetery, the storekeeper told him that Haycock was very much alive.

Subsequent investigations led to a happy reunion at Jonesport with Haycock, his 73-year-old mother and other members of her family. "It was the biggest thrill of my life," the seaman said. "I didn't know my mother was alive."

This tangle resulted from a storm in 1903 which claimed the life of William Winchester, a Bluenose fisherman. He left a widow and two children, Florence, six, and Carleton, three. Ill and unable to support two children, Mrs. Winchester placed her son for adoption with an agency. He was adopted by Capt. and Mrs. Gus Haycock, of Digby, N. S. They raised him as their child, in Digby and Westport, and he never learned his true identity.

At 15, young Haycock added three years to his age and joined the 64th Battalion. After eight months basic training, he transferred to the 85th Highlanders and sailed overseas in October, 1916. In October, 1917, Pte. Carleton Haycock was wounded in action at Passchendaele. "We really got cut up. Only 150 survived from our battalion of 900," he recalled.

Suffering from machine-gun wounds in both legs, the young soldier played dead until nightfall and then crawled to a first-aid station behind his own lines. Through an error, the government notified his foster parents that he was missing in action. The mistake was discovered and, a month later, the earlier report was corrected. Meanwhile, Haycock's real mother, who had been informed by Mrs. Haycock of the first report, moved to the United States and remarried. She was unaware that the erroneous report had been contradicted.

After seven months in hospital, Haycock returned home. Capt. Haycock had died during the war period and, as far as Carleton knew, Mrs. Haycock was his only relative. When she died in January, 1945, he believed he was an orphan.

Following his discharge, Haycock worked on the construction of a dam for the Nova Scotia Power Commission. But his war injuries left him less nimble on his feet. One day a huge hemlock piling fell toward him and he couldn't move fast enough. He sustained a smashed foot. Just out of hospital, he was alighting from a Halifax street car when it lurched. Trying to save himself, he broke his left arm when he hit the street.

The jinx followed him after he joined the marine service of the Imperial Oil Co. in October, 1923. His legs, which still bear evidence of his war wounds, still weren't back to par. On shore leave early in his seafaring career, he turned up a dark alley one night, fell into an open pit and dislocated his shoulder. Later, while serving in the Montrolite, someone left off a plate in the pump room, exposing an eight-foot hole. Haycock found it the hard way and suffered several broken ribs.

The legend that he is virtually indestructible stems from these mishaps and the fact that he survived three tanker collisions and a torpedoing. The worst of the collisions occured three years ago at the River Plate when the Imperial Quebec and another tanker crashed in a fog. Fortunately, a smouldering fire aboard the Quebec was quickly brought under control and only one crew member was badly burned. But it took three months in drydock to plug the 150-foot hole in the tanker's side.

The torpedoing was Haycock's worst experience. He was one of 20 survivors of a crew of 48. It was the night of Feb. 4, 1942. The Imperial Montrolite was running without lights from Port of Spain, Trinidad, to Halifax with a full cargo of oil. It was 8 o'clock. Haycock, a pumpman in the Montrolite, was aft with his shipmates listening to a broadcast.

"We felt a heavy jar and then there was the awful smell of cordite," Haycock recalled. "A sheet of flame shot up higher than the mast. We knew it was a torpedo and we wanted to get off before she caught fire or sank. It was a stormy night and we had lashed the lifeboats to the deck that afternoon. I don't know how we ever got them away. Three men got off in one boat and we never saw them again. Capt. Jack White and 24 others were in the other boat and they were lost, too."

Haycock recalls jumping into a sea of oil "a foot thick." He said his eyes were full of oil but he managed to see a lifeboat near and swam toward it. "I didn't know it at the time but the doctors think I must have broken my neck when I hit the water. I remember my head hitting my life preserver with an awful jolt."

Friendly hands pulled him into the lifeboat which contained 19 other crew members. "We pulled up around the tanker into the wind," he said. "Then the second torpedo hit her and she caught fire. I like to think the U-boat commander gave us a chance. The last we saw of our ship she was lying on her stern. We were in the lifeboat from Wednesday night until Saturday afternoon, when we were picked up by an English freighter which was bound from St. Lucia to Halifax. By this time we were getting pretty weak. We were cold and wet and had to keep bailing all the time. It was stormy all the time, and shortly before we were picked up it started to get worse. I didn't think we were going to be able to get aboard the freighter: We finally made it and they gave us hot soup, rum, and some coffee. The Atlantic can be pretty grim in February and that night was the worst storm of all. We wouldn't have lived through it."

After this experience, he suffered from severe head-aches. He said he was in hospital three times before the cause was determined. In 1945, doctors at the Montreal General Hospital discovered he had a broken neck. "The injury was too close to a nerve for them to operate," he said. "It's all right as long as I don't do too much lifting."

When he got the first letter from his mother, Haycock said he didn't believe it. "I thought it was just a gag. But it turned out to be the truth. I went to Jonesport and saw her and we had lots to talk over. We write each other all the time now. This summer we're planning a real family reunion in Nova Scotia. My sister, Florence, lives at Canso. I'll see her this summer, too."

13

MY 69 HOURS OF HELL

Louis Jaques Photo

Fishing skipper Alden Locke, of Jordan Bay, N.S., is reunited with his family after three days adrift in the cold, stormy sea. He tells of ordeal that claimed mate's life.

The worst 69 hours of my life began shortly after 7 o'clock on the Tuesday night when I heard my shipmate, Jim Stewart, yelling. I'd been asleep for about an hour in the cuddy (cabin) of my boat, the Caroline And Eric. I can't just say Jim's words — I guess I wasn't quite awake — but it was something about water.

Jim sounded pretty excited, so I guessed we must be in some kind of trouble. Then I noticed an inch or so of water on the cud floor. It was rising. We were in trouble, all right!

We'd been fishing on Little La Have, about 45 miles offshore, and had begun to head back for Shelburne with a good catch of 7,500 pounds. On the way in we dressed

89

our fish and had supper. Then I went in the cuddy for an hour and a half's sleep. After that I was going to relieve Jim at the wheel. We expected to be home early Wednesday morning. Just a routine trip, I thought. I couldn't have been more wrong.

The sight of that water on the cud floor brought me to my senses. Just then, from somewheres aft, I heard Jim holler, "My God! We're sinking!"

I ran aft and was just abreast of the engine when it stopped. I started to chuck a couple of fish overboard in a feeble effort to lighten her. There was two feet of water in the stern and it suddenly went right under, just as if the sea was breaking into her.

I ran back to the cuddy and grabbed the mike. I got out the "May Day" three times and said, "We're sinking!" Then the radio went under water. I got out of the cud just in time, crawled forward on top of the windshield and looked around for Jim. I saw him hanging on the aft end, in the water. He called out, "I can't get up!"

I yelled to him to hang on a minute, waded back, grabbed him by the shirt and helped him aboard. We both got up by the windshield. "What on earth happened?" I asked.

Jim didn't know exactly. "It all happened so fast," he said. We figured that fish guts and bait must have caught in the scupper holes of the self-bailing fish hold and plugged them. When we have a load, the water comes in the rudder port and drains off through the scuppers. When she's steaming along, she keeps herself dry. It's a freak accident to have all eight scupper holes get plugged up. But that's what must have happened. She just filled up and sank until she was almost completely under the water.

It wasn't stormy — just a little chop and a five-mile wind. The water was cold and we weren't dressed for it. Just pants and shirt. I didn't even have a pair of shoes. We were 27 miles sou'-sou'-east of Shelburne.

"I got a message away," I told Jim. "If it got through there's a chance we'll be found — if we don't sink first."

In about 15 or 20 minutes the chop of the sea worked loose the windshield, which was flush with the water, and it drifted away. We crawled back on top of the pilot house. Everything loose had started to come out of her as soon as she went down — fish, buoys, trawl tubs. When the waves hit the cuddy windows she would rock, so we broke out the windows to let the seas through and steady her. We edged toward the back part of the cuddy and tied ourselves to the window frames so we wouldn't be washed overboard if a big wave came.

About an hour before daylight on Wednesday, I saw the lights of two vessels, one on either side of us. We both watched them until they got closer and then we yelled for help. But they were too far off to hear us and it was too dark to see us because we had no light. If it had been daylight one of them would have spotted us, I'm sure. They went by without stopping. I think they were fishing vessels.

After that we saw an airplane to east'ard, but it was quite a ways off and didn't see us. Then we saw a steamer two or three miles off. We could see her but she couldn't see us.

All Wednesday morning it was fine and clear, but we were very cold from standing in water below our hips. The cramps in our legs got so bad we didn't think we could stand it. We rubbed our stomachs and our legs and kind of moved around a bit but it didn't seem to do much good. We prayed a bit. "Please, God," we prayed, "send a boat to pick us up."

Around noon I saw the fog. It hung over the coast and was moving slowly toward us. "It's going to shut down thick," I told Jim. We both knew what that could mean.

"It's an awful thing," Jim said, "for people ashore

to let us die this way. I don't believe anyone is coming to look for us."

"You never know, Jim," I said. "There might be 10 or 15 boats out looking for us. One might come along."

But I wasn't feeling too hopeful. It seemed like everything was against us. When a boat did come it was too far off to find us. And now the fog made it that much worse. The fog was our main worry now. We knew it was going to shut down and we prayed we'd be found before it did.

No such luck. The fog closed in and by early afternoon was very thick. We didn't think our chances were very good then. Not unless a boat spotted us on its radar screen.

"Maybe it'll clear tomorrow. They'll have no chance findin' us in this," I said.

Jim told me, "I don't know whether I can hang on that long."

I said I didn't know if I could either.

After that we just waited and hoped. We went for hours without saying a word. There was nothing to talk about.

It was still thick the next morning — Thursday. That morning, before daylight, a boat went by us. We heard her engine and we felt her wake but we never seen her. We hollered again but she never heard us.

Around noon on Thursday it cleared up so we could see for a couple of miles. Then we saw a black boat go by us. We waved and called but she didn't see us. She was a little bigger than a dragger — maybe a search vessel. A short time later two steamers went up on the other side of us. They didn't see us either. Then it shut down thick again and we couldn't see nowheres.

Around 4 o'clock that afternoon, she went down a foot and a half deeper. It must have been the tide that brung her down. The water was now up to our armpits. Jim tried to get higher by crawling toward the windshield but he was too weak. The motion of the boat threw him off balance and he fell over backwards into the sea. He was still tied to the boat and I managed to pull him back aboard. He had quite a bit of water in him and he vomited when he got back on his feet again. He had lost his glasses and his cap.

I could see that Jim was getting weaker. The chops were coming about two feet high, and we'd have to hold our breath when they broke over our heads. Sometimes they'd knock us over. Jim was game but he was having a hard time to get back on his feet. When the waves hit him he'd fall down on his knees with his face in the water and I'd help him up. He'd kinda groan and gag when he got water in him. He vomited a few times more.

Jim said, "I don't think I can hold on any longer. In this fog they won't have any chance of finding us anyway. You might be picked up but I won't."

We'd been in the water for over 45 hours without being found and I wasn't very hopeful now. "It doesn't look like I'm going to be picked up either," I told him. "I'll probably hold on for quite a while yet if she doesn't sink completely. I've still got a little strength in my arms but my legs are stiff."

Jim didn't last long after that. The last time a chop hit him I tried to get him back on his feet but he couldn't help himself. He didn't move at all, so I knew he was gone. I had known him about 15 years and we had fished together a lot. It was awful to see a good friend go like that.

Jim died at about a quarter to five. After he died, I thought to myself: *The boat's going to sink. With that and the thick fog, I won't have a chance.* But after an hour and a half she came back up a piece. The tide must have slackened some. I thought: *When the tide turns tomorrow morning before daylight, she'll sink for sure.*

But she didn't go down any deeper. When daylight came Friday she came up right good. The fog cleared and

and it got fine and pretty near calm. I had tied myself to three different parts of the boat to hold myself up. I knew I had to keep awake.

I don't know whether I was dreaming or not, but at times I thought there was someone there talking to me. It was so real once when I heard this talking that I was sure a man was there. He was steering a punt and came alongside so I could get in. I untied the ropes and started to get in the punt. Then I realized that there wasn't any punt there and that I was just imagining it. I got the ropes and tied myself again.

Around 2 o'clock Friday a plane came. It was like someone told me it was there. This voice said, "There's a plane there but I suppose she won't come down here." I hadn't seen the plane before this. Now I looked up and saw it circling around. The plane must have seen something on the water. I waved to them and they waved back. Then they dropped a flare and I knew then they'd send for help. Then two more airplanes came and one dropped a raft with some emergency food, but it drifted away.

I never seen the rescue boat until she was about up to me. I looked around and the boat was there. They put a lifeboat over the side and got me and Jim's body. It was all over – the worst 69 hours of my life.

14

MEN AGAINST THE WILD ATLANTIC

On a bitterly cold night in January, the little fishing vessel Robert and Brian fouled a reef four miles off Isaac's Harbor, N.S., and began breaking up in a 35-m.p.h. Atlantic storm. The time was 1:30 A. M.

Capt. Stewart Demone, 44, of Lunenburg, N.S. the vessel's skipper, who had been sailing since his teens, knew that neither he nor the three other crew members would stand a chance if help failed to arrive soon. He got off a frantic S O S. Then the radio went dead. The four men holed up in the wheelhouse where they waited and prayed.

By 4:30 the wind and the sea had battered the wheelhouse to rubble, leaving the men exposed to the elements. The cold was intense.

"She's breaking in two!" one of the quartet shouted. Capt. Demone ordered all to go aft. He and crewman Earl Forward, 25, of Harbor Grace, Nfld., jumped and made it. Their craft was now in two pieces. Eric Fanning, 20, of Little Dover, N.S., and Watson Knickle, 16, of Lunenburg, jumped too late and fell into the icy sea.

By a superhuman effort, Capt. Demone managed to get within reach of the struggling pair and pulled them to safety. The feat was performed at great personal risk. Four hours later, the half-dozen men were rescued by the United States fishing dragger St. Nicholas. This took great courage on the part of Capt. Thomas Barisi and his crew. The sea was at the doomed ship's deck level when the four were hauled aboard the dragger by a lifeline.

Maritime history is studded with feats of great heroism by men whose valor often gets no more recognition than a newspaper headline — and sometimes not that. The men who put to sea in small vessels, particularly in winter, face perils unknown to those on land. The enemy is the sea. It's a constant enemy. In this age of sea giants, atomic submarines and modern mechanical means of navigation, there are still little vessels at sea facing the same perils and hardships as the seamen of the past.

The 324-ton trawler Cape Agulhas groped through a dense pre-dawn fog the morning of Jan.6, 1956, home-ward-bound to Halifax with 120,000 pounds of fish in her holds. A chill breeze swept over the dark, heaving Atlantic. In almost 20 years of plying between Halifax and the fishing grounds, the sturdy vessel had faced plenty of fog and bad weather. But today the problem was more serious. Her radar and sounding equipment were out of order.

Capt. Jack Lilly, of Halifax, the skipper, knew the danger of "flying blind" through fog that thick. It clung about his ship like a clammy shroud, reducing visibility to a mere 30 feet. The skipper, in whose hands lay the safety of his ship and crew of 17, peered anxiously from the bridge. He reduced speed to three knots.

Down below, Ernest Thornhill, 30, of West Dover,N.S., the trawler's big, barrel-chested mate, had stirred from his bunk and was coming aloft to stand the 6 A.M. watch. Like others of the crew, he was looking forward to a spell ashore with his wife and five children.

Thornhill had taken only a few paces when suddenly the Cape Agulhas came to a dead stop with a crash. The jar threw the mate off balance. He righted himself and scrambled toward the bridge. Capt. Lilly met him half-way. "We're aground," he announced grimly.

The trawler lay on a rocky ledge about 40 yards off

Portuguese Cove. Fog and darkness blotted out the nearby coast but those aboard the doomed ship could plainly hear the breakers pounding against the jagged shoreline. Excited crewmen poured on deck and tried desperately to launch the lifeboats. But the trawler was breaking up too fast in the rough seas and they abandoned the effort.

The captain and mate dashed to the bow and made a hasty survey of their plight. Water was pouring in through a gaping hole in the trawler's hull. The captain grabbed a lifeline. "If we could only get this line ashore, we could get everyone off. It's our only chance," he said.

Thornhill kicked off his boots. "Let me try," he volunteered. There was no time to waste. The captain wrapped the line twice around Thornhill's waist. Then the mate plunged into the water and struck out toward shore.

The heroic fisherman's memory of his swim ashore is hazy. He was soon lost from the view of the others on the sinking ship. The last they saw of him, he was making headway in the direction of the coast. Thornhill's most vivid recollection of that swim was when a great comber hurled him toward the rugged shore and his foot struck a protruding rock, fracturing his heel. The stabbing pain that shot through his leg was almost unbearable. He managed to yell back to the ship, "I'm hurt!" Unable to stand, he clutched at clumps of seaweed to keep himself from being sucked back into the sea by the backwash and managed to pull himself ashore.

The cold, weary fishermen now had a new problem. There was no suitable anchoring place near him for the lifeline. Desperately, he looked for a rock. He spotted one part-way up the hill. The fear that he might be too late to save his companions spurred him on as he began crawling toward it, dragging his useless leg.

When he reached his goal, he almost blacked out from pain and exhaustion. Laboriously, he began to circle the rock. When he came back to where he saw the smudges of his knees in the mud of the bank — the starting point — he made the line fast. All the ship's crew came ashore safely via the lifeline. The rescue was completed just in time. As the last man was coming ashore, the trawler broke up and sank in 50 feet of water. Just before it disappeared, fellow crewmen carried Thornhill over the bank to escape a possible boiler explosion.

Six weeks earlier, two Royal Canadian Navy helicopter pilots displayed great courage off the coast of Cape Breton when they rescued 21 Greek seamen from the Liberian freighter Kismet II. For 29 hours, the crew had clung to their wrecked ship at Cape St. Lawrence. The doomed vessel lay at the foot of a 400-foot overhanging cliff which thwarted rescue efforts from ashore.

The heroes of this drama were Lt.-Cmdr. Jack Beaman, of Montreal, and Lt.-Cmdr. Roger Finck, of Ponoka, Alta. They took turns guiding the helicopter down to the deck of the stricken ship, the aircraft's whirling blades at times only a few feet away from the cliff face. Holding the helicopter steady in the 25 m.p.h.-wind and setting it down on the small, cleared portion of the ship's deck, called for great skill and courage.

The helicopter crew took four trips to complete the rescue, one of the most dramatic recorded on the Atlantic seaboard in recent years. Some of the rescued seamen were so over-come with emotion they kissed members of the aircraft crew.

Sometimes the drama may have a heroine.

The flying boat Cavalier was on a routine flight to Bermuda with 13 passengers and crew. The weather was clear for the take-off and early part of the flight. But, suddenly, out over the Atlantic, a freak storm of hail and snow began. The aircraft's wings were soon heavily coated and it began to lose altitude rapidly. A steward, who was well aware of the danger, said calmly, "We're going to land for lunch. Fasten your seat belts."

There was, of course, no lunch. And no safe place

to land. The Cavalier was 300 miles southeast of Cape May, N.J. In the murk below lay only the storm-churned ocean. The flying boat came down fast. Then there was a terrific crash and the plane's bottom seemed to be breaking up. Its occupants scrambled through doors and hatches and plunged into the sea. They had only minutes to escape. Two male passengers were drowned in the attempt. The others – five men and five women – clung to the few salvaged life preservers. The Cavalier sank from sight.

The pilot, Capt. R. M. Alderson, lost consciousness and started to sink. A woman near him grabbed his tunic and held him afloat. She was Mrs. Edna Watson, an ex-Montrealer who had been returning to her home in Bermuda. Mrs. Watson held the pilot above water for over an hour until he revived. At this point sharks were spotted in the vicinity and one of the women became hysterical. Mrs. Watson quieted her.

Close to midnight, the tanker Esso Baytown, commanded by Capt. Frank H. Spurr, arrived on the scene and dispatched a life-boat to rescue the weary survivors. For her bravery during this ordeal and for helping to keep up the courage of her companions, Mrs. Watson was awarded the Royal Humane Society's Silver Medal.

Many other feats of heroism worthy of medals go unnoticed by the world . . . A lifeboat puts into angry forbidding waters, manned by a crew who risk death to save shipwrecked men, women, and children.   A courageous wireless operator remains at his post to the last, tapping out the call for help which may mean the salvation of passengers and crew in his sinking vessel . . . The band-master of the S. S. Titanic calmly waves his baton and the band strikes up Nearer My God To Thee as the liner sinks and over 1,500 perish . . . A seaman voluntarily plunges into shark-infested seas to rescue a shipmate who has been washed overboard . . . A weary, half-frozen Bluenose sea captain mumbles the last rites for a dying shipmate. Then he goes back to the herculean task of rowing endless miles through a Bay of Fundy blizzard in a futile attempt to save the lifeboat survivors.

Turn back the calendar to a cold, stormy day in February, 1949. The 29-ton Lunenburg fishing dragger Brenda Marie is trapped on a ledge of rock off Isaac's Harbor Light near the northern tip of the Nova Scotia mainland. All through the night and early morning, seven men have clung to their ship as wave after wave threatened to sweep them overboard. It is now late morning and, after 12 hours on the ledge, the dragger's bottom is holed through and she is breaking up. In that awful sea, she can't last much longer. And there is no rescue ship near.

"We've got one chance — get a line ashore." The speaker is Capt. Orlando "Land" Lace, Jr., 22, of Lunenburg, skipper of the dragger Brenda Marie. It isn't much of a chance. The course from ship to shore is a raging patch of ocean and the finish line a jagged series of menacing rocks against which the surf hammers relentlessly. A man could easily drown in that sea. Or he might cover the distance and be dashed to death against the rocks. But it's a chance.

"I'll try, sir." The volunteer is Seaman Joseph Fry, a weather-bronzed young fisherman. His shipmates fasten a line about him and he leaps into the sea. A wave catches him and he disappears. He reappears and strikes out for shore. But the courageous swimmer is battling hopeless odds. After a short, unsuccessful struggle, it is quite evident he can't make it. His shipmates pull him back aboard the Brenda Marie and he slumps on deck, chilled through, half-drowned and completely exhausted.

The seas lift the dragger and drop her on the rocks again and again. She is taking water fast. The grim-faced skipper slips the lifeline from Fry's waist and puts it around his own. He poises momentarily at the ship's rail, studying the action of the waves, and then plunges into the sea.

The lives of seven men hang on the outcome of this

100

swim. Land Lace's plunge carries him away from the ship. A huge wave catches his body, spins him, and flings him back – perilously close to the dragger. He strikes out for shore again and his shipmates pay out the lifeline which snakes behind him in the seething seas.

The swimmer rides the crest of a mighty breaker and is lost in its trough. He reappears, still swimming, then disappears once more. It's a heartbreaking struggle. Time after time, the sea beats the swimmer back. But, gradually, the determined man narrows the gap between himself and the shore. But his strength is waning. He is now near the coast. His companions aboard the dragger lose sight of him completely as a great wave engulfs him. Seconds later – it seems like an eternity – he is on the surface again, almost within reach of the rocky shore. And then, miraculously, Land Lace has accomplished the seemingly impossible. He is ashore. He staggers to his feet, stumbles through the breakers to a point above the waterline, and secures the lifeline. Two hours later, his six companions have come hand over hand down the lifeline to safety.

The heroic actions of Land Lace and Ernest Thornhill were in the tradition laid down by such classic heroes as Quartermaster Speakman of the S.S. Atlantic. When the ship ran aground on the rocky shore near Peggy's Cove, N.S., on March 20, 1873, little hope was held for her 931 passengers and crew. But Speakman swam heroically through the surf. Exhausted and bleeding, he managed to gain a rock and hold on until the sea receded. Then he scrambled ashore with a lifeline which resulted in the rescue of most of the 300 survivors.

Early in May of 1955, the British freighter S.S. Kildale was steaming leisurely across the Atlantic on her way from Cornwall, England, to Three Rivers, Que., with a cargo of china clay. Down in the engine room, among the tangle of pipes and the noise of throbbing pistons, the air was hot and filled with the strong, dank smell of oil.

Among the lower-deck crew on watch this night was Edward McGowan, a native of Liverpool, the ship's donkeyman. McGowan was a veteran of 34 years at sea. He had survived two torpedoings in World War II and the Normandy beach-head landings.

Shortly after McGowan came on watch, the heat in the engine room seemed to become more intense. Looking up, he noticed flames and dense smoke coming from atop the main boilers. McGowan yelled "Fire!" Then, seizing a fire extinguisher, he scaled the steel ladder and, despite the intense heat, quelled the blaze single handed. After that the exhausted donkeyman then started down the ladder to the deck below. As he did so the ship rolled slowly in the ocean swell. The oil that had originally started the fire came in contact with the hot pipes again, burst into flames and poured down on the descending man. McGowan screamed in agony, lost his footing and fell all the way to the lower deck.

The engineer and other helpers leaped toward the injured man and were able to smother the flames which enveloped his body. Then they started to peel off the burned clothing. Large patches of skin came off with the clothes and his whole body was blackened. He was not expected to live. The ship was then 150 miles from Sydney and made an 18-hour dash into port where the heroic seaman recovered after many weeks of hospital treatment.

The nightmarish voyage of 12 men and a woman in a lifeboat during a Bay of Fundy blizzard in February, 1946, graphically illustrates the amazing courage and endurance which some people display in an emergency. The 13 in the lifeboat were the survivors in the 265-ton freighter Robert G. Cann, which had gone down eight miles off Grand Manan soon after the storm struck.

"I've never seen seas so big nor felt such intense cold," recalled Capt. Arthur Ells, mate of the vessel, who took charge of the rescue attempt. "Our lifeboat was just a living foam all the time and the roar of the wind and seas drowned out everything. Everyone was too numb to talk, sing, or even pray. We did everything in our power to keep out the cold — huddling together, moving our limbs. But it was of no use."

For 19½ hours, Ells and Seaman Joseph Muise stuck to the oars in a superhuman effort to reach shore. The prevailing wind carried them far across the bay toward the Nova Scotia shore. The temperature was five below zero. Waters kept breaking over the lifeboat whose occupants became colder and colder. Mrs. Lawrence Jacquard, a stewardess, huddled in the stern alongside her husband, the ship's cook.

As Ells and Muise rowed, the others bailed. The boat was taking in a lot of water and was in danger of being swamped. The vapor, the snow and the darkness made it impossible for those in the boat to see ahead. They had an added worry. They lacked horns and lights to signal the lifeboat's position, increasing the danger of being cut down by a passing ship.

Then, one by one, the occupants of the lifeboat died. The first to go was Capt. Frank Peters, who had a bad heart. He died at 6 A.M., about two hours after entering the lifeboat. Ells left his place at the oars long enough to say a prayer for him. Lawrence Jacquard died at 8 A.M. His face was frozen and he went fast. His wife was beside him but she thought he was just asleep. Nobody told her the truth. The cold grew more intense. As each man died, Ells said a prayer for him. Lou David, Fitzgerald, Bent, Davis, Tommy Bartlett, a young Indian deck hand, and Chief Engineer Harry Logan. Some were married men with families. Others were single. There were now nine dead. Four clung to life.

Ells and Muise continued to row with the desperation of men facing almost certain death. With their waning strength, those in the lifeboat chopped away the ice which weighed down the small craft and threatened to sink it.

They had no food or water. Toward evening the weather cleared but the cold was just as intense. Away in the distance loomed Boar's Head on the Nova Scotia coast. Ells leaned over to tell Mrs. Jacquard the good news. "I can't stand it any longer," she mumbled. She died while he was talking to her. George Pendrick, the ship's fireman, died a few minutes later. Then Muise slumped over his oar — too cold and too far gone to row another stroke.

It was almost midnight when the frail, ice-burdened lifeboat reached the beach at Riley's Cove with its 11 dead and two near death. Ells staggered a short distance up the beach, dragging Muise with him. He knew his companion would die if he didn't get help quickly. Ells left Muise on the beach and went for aid. At the end of a moonlit wagon track he came to a house and brought first word of the tragedy. A rescue party found Muise on the beach but he died en route to hospital. Ells, miraculously, recovered.

It would take volumes to pay even partial tribute to the many who have risked their lives in valiant efforts to save others at sea. When the liner Morro Castle caught fire in September, 1934, off the coast of New Jersey, Chief Radio Operator George Rogers remained at his key amid the blistering heat, tapping out the S O S until shipmates forcibly removed him. When the tanker Pendleton sank in a gale off Cape Cod in February, 1952, a four-man lifeboat crew saved 32 survivors at the risk of being capsized in heavy seas. Thirty-one Portuguese fishermen owe their lives to a heroic lifeboat crew from the United States transport Stafford. This crew made two round trips through 40-foot seas to rescue them from the sinking schooner Maria Carlota during a storm off the Grand Banks in November, 1947.

Sometimes the principals in these epic rescues have received due recognition for their heroism. Often their feats have gone unrewarded. It's all in the proud tradition of men against the sea. For many who gave their lives there is not even an epitaph.

15

ADMIRAL OF THE SALVAGE FLEET

Capt. Bob Featherstone, a rugged, ruddy-faced marine salvage master of Halifax, has spent the bulk of his 54 years robbing Davy Jones.

In an adventure-packed 34 years at his hazardous profession, the cigar-chewing, 190-pound admiral of the Foundation Maritime Co. ocean-going salvage fleet has had spectacular success. He has refloated some ships which were so hard aground it required a bulldozer to help pry them off the shore.

Featherstone holds a decoration from the King of Belgium for his part in clearing the harbors of Zeebrugge and Ostend of concrete-filled British cruisers sunk in World War I to bottle up the German U-boat fleet; a citation from the British Admirality for saving valuable shipping in the big fire at Southampton in 1922, and the MBE for his share in the Battle of the Atlantic.

Since the war he has added to this record, an outstanding recent feat being the refloating of the 20,175-ton Cunard Donaldson liner Franconia from a rocky ledge in the St. Lawrence river last July.

"He has the uncanny knack of determining within a few minutes whether a ship is salvageable," commented Ed Turner, the Foundation Co. secretary-treasurer and long-time co-worker with Featherstone in the Halifax office. "If the Cap says he can't get a ship off, then nothing in God's half acre will ever get it off."

Throughout the length and breadth of the North Atlantic he is known as the master of the fast pull-off, a capable sea lawyer, and a tough negotiator who, within seconds of his arrival at the scene of a casualty, can clinch a favorable deal for his company with the ship's master.

One-time officer-in-charge of the Admiralty Salvage Section in England, Featherstone is today key man in a marine salvage organization which in the past 18 years has salvaged more than $200,000,000 in ships and cargo and saved London underwriters over half that amount in seagoing insurance claims.

On a difficult job when human life and millions of dollars in shipping and cargo are at stake, this Sunderland-born blue-eyed Englishman is as placid as if he were at home poring over his prized collection of stamps. He is the direct antithesis of the ranting, hell-raising skipper who bellows commands from the bridge. Featherstone gives his orders in little more than a whisper, surveying the work of his crack salvage crew with all the appearance of a mildly interested spectator.

On many a job Featherstone has been dunked in the sea. A strong swimmer, he has always managed to scramble

107

to safety, cigar still fast in the side of his mouth. The heater is standard equipment. On a tough job he will chain-smoke, or chew, as many as 20 a day. A bulldog endurance enables him to keep on his feet from 24 to 36 hours or more without evidence of fatigue. Then, after a cat nap, he'll be back on deck as fresh as ever.

Physically, he's as solid as a ship's anchor. An amateur boxer in young days, he still knows how to use his fists but never does. He is proud of the fact that he weathered scores of bouts aboard ship or in dozens of ports of the world without suffering a KO or a black eye.

The attitude of his men toward their boss is akin to hero-worship. It's a Featherstone rule never to ask a man to do a job he wouldn't do himself, whether it be shovelling coal to keep up steam in a crippled ship or fighting fire on a blazing tanker. When the job is particularly dangerous, Featherstone calls for volunteers. He leads the way himself and when the mission is completed sees that his crews are paid a generous bonus.

Featherstone, who takes a fatherly interest in his salvage teams, will never send a diver below without having a companion ready to replace him if he gets into trouble. He is justifiably proud of his safety record, and has never lost a man on a job.

Nowadays, Featherstone spends more time in his office which overlooks Halifax harbor than he does afloat. But he has never lost his love of the sea. He frequently beats his own tugs to the scene of a wreck, travelling by airplane or by car. He doesn't like air travel and confesses he would feel more secure below surface in a submarine than above it in an aircraft.

Friends who draw him into conversation hoping to hear some dramatic yarn about his damp and dangerous career are apt to be disappointed. To him, raising ships from the deep, snatching them from reefs or pulling them to port through howling nor'easters is all in the day's work. He'd as soon talk about his stamps or his animals.

108

The Featherstone menagerie of cats and dogs is out of this world, which is where some of his neighbors wish it were, literally. He has a penchant for police dogs. In his comfortable frame house on the outskirts of Dartmouth, he has had as many as 15 cats and two or more dogs at one time.

On occasions his dogs go driving with the Cap. His friends say this proves they are dumb animals. Of Featherstone's car-driving ability, or lack of it, an acquaintance remarked: "He doesn't feel a car is properly broken in until it's minus a couple of fenders." After one accident he lost his licence for a month. He has reportedly driven hell-bent down the town's sidewalks in winter when the middle of the street was unplowed.

His habit of fast driving is often in the call of duty. A telephone is within arm's length of his bed. "It rings at the damnedest hours. When a ship is in distress you've got to act fast. Minutes count in the salvage game," he explained. Within 15 minutes after an urgent call summoning him to a wreck along the coast, Featherstone is on the road, throttle well open.

"Speed," he says, "is essential in this job. You've usually got to get a ship off in three or four days or she'll suffer so much damage she'll break up."

That might well have been the fate of the Franconia after it piled atop two reefs off the Island of Orleans just below Quebec last July. Even before his company was given the job, Featherstone and his salvage crew were headed there by train.

They found the liner so hard aground that guests at an island hotel had hurriedly removed their cars from the wharf which they feared the Franconia was going to demolish as it ground on the rocky beach. Before Featherstone's men got there, others had made a futile attempt to free the ship.

Featherstone sized up the job within minutes. Long before his tugboats arrived, he had worked out a plan to

109

correct the vessel's eight degree list and pull her off the shelf. The night before the big pull, he telephoned the company president, Richard E. Chadwick, at Montreal, and Turner at Halifax. "I'll have her off at seven-thirty tomorrow morning," he promised.

Company officials have long since ceased being astounded by the way their salvage chief calls his shots. True to his word, at the predicted hour Featherstone had the Franconia afloat. The entire job had taken 40 hours, an unusually short time for a salvage undertaking of that size.

Featherstone's salvage crew refloated the Franconia on the highest tide of the month. They distributed the water in her ballast tanks to right her, pumped compressed air into her to lighten her. Seven tugs and river craft took part in the big pull, the liner's own winches exerting a pull on ground tackle and salvage anchors equal to that of eight tugs.

"It would have been fatal to wait for another period of high tide. She'd probably have broken up. Besides," grinned Featherstone, "I was booked to sail for England on the Ascania two days later, so I had to get her off then or miss the trip."

Around the Halifax office, Turner still chuckles over the day he called Featherstone into his office and dumped a seemingly impossible problem into the salvage master's lap.

The British steamship Lackenby, 5,002 tons, had grounded on the southwest tip of Bell Island, Newfoundland, in September, 1937. The vessel's skipper, Ben Moss, had radioed his owners: "There's no doubt I'm a total loss." Marine records showed that, once set ashore on this dangerous stretch of the Newfoundland coast, few ships had ever been refloated. According to information from the scene, the Lackenby was fast on two jagged reefs with a four-degree list, holed through fore and aft, her holds and engine room flooded. To complicate matters, a 220-foot cliff rose sheer from the sea, offering no foot-hold for salvage teams to work from shore. The tide, so often an ally of the salvage man, had a mere two-foot range at this point, and the weather was foul.

"Looks pretty hopeless, eh?" queried Turner.

Featherstone said, "Hmmm." He glanced at the calendar. He pulled out a cigar, lit it and pondered a few moments. He was conjuring up a mental picture of a dis-tressed ship, 600 miles away on a stormswept reef.

"Tell you what I'll do, Ed," said Featherstone at length. "This one will be a bit difficult. I'll have the Lackenby out of there between eleven and twelve on Sunday night, October tenth, and I'll send you a wire to confirm it."

Turner, who is a close personal friend of Feather-stone's and frequently bets with him on the time a job will take, wagered a bottle of rum on the Lackenby job.

"I thought I'd nick the Cap for sure on this one," said Turner, "but I'll be damned if he didn't pull the Lackenby off exactly on the day and hour he named. That's one bet I cheerfully lost."

When he looks back on the Lackenby assignment, Featherstone remembers it as a two-week nightmare. On numerous occasions the seas almost wrecked the motor-boat carrying salvage workers, pumps and compressors to the grounded ship. Great walls of surf constantly broke over the vessel, at times forcing a halt to operations. Twice the pitch of the seas nearly wrecked one of the salvage craft, once when a bower anchor plunged into her bulwarks and again when a bower anchor, swinging in a great haymaker, almost carried away her forward saloon. Throughout, the Lackenby's tortured hull creaked and groaned as the seas bumped her and ground her on her rocky perch. As new leaks opened up, divers went below to patch them. Pumped dry, her coal bunkers jettisoned, the sturdy salvage tug Foundation Franklin pulling in a clear patch of sea ahead, and pulled by her own bootstraps, the freighter came off one ledge. Featherstone then ordered her forward hold flooded to tip the bow and, with the next combined pull by the tug, and the ship's own engines, the Lackenby was freed off the second ledge. Heading for drydock in St. John's, she beat out a storm which might well have sent her to the bottom had she been aground at the time.

The twin attributes of daring and ingenuity help explain Featherstone's unique record. Like many a mariner, he admits he's a fatalist. "I'll get it when my number's up," he says, never worrying about the prospect.

He nearly got it one day during the removal of a cargo of 750 blockbusters from the US Liberty ship William Maclay, aground on Elbow Shoal, at the southwestern tip of Nova Scotia. Featherstone's men were transferring these bombs from a pitching and rolling lighter to the hold of a Norwegian ship. The Cap was on the deck of the Norse ship, supervising the job. Every now and again one of the bombs would break loose and crash into the others.

Suddenly the cantankerous ship's winch reversed while lowering a blockbuster, twirled this package of sudden death about the derrick head, and snapped the wires that held it. As the bomb fell 60 feet straight down into sufficient other blockbusters to make a sizable dent in Berlin, Featherstone and his crew held their breath and waited for the deck to blow up under them. Miraculously, the bomb neither exploded nor plowed through the vessel's bottom. "I still can't figure why," says the still perplexed salvage chief.

It's an ironic touch in the Featherstone saga that this salvage expert who was to play so vital a role in the war against the Axis was rescued from almost certain death by the Japanese.

The British steamship Berwindlea had grounded in October, 1935, on a Magdelen Island shoal off Dead Man's Island. A storm broke the vessel's back and marooned a Featherstone-led salvage party aboard. For two awful days and nights they clung to the ship which mountainous seas threatened to sink. The Foundation Franklin tried to fire a lifeline aboard but couldn't get in close enough. The ship's crew and the Franklin tried to launch lifeboats, which were ground to bits on the rocks. At this point the Japanese cargo vessel came steaming to the rescue and, with the Franklin forming a lea, removed the salvage crew, officers and men in two daring trips by lifeboat. Within hours of the rescue the seas smashed the Berwindlea to splinters and it sank in 16 fathoms of boiling surf.

Featherstone's love of the sea is in the family tradition. Both his father and grandfather were seafaring men. With the able help of his Uncle George, a North Sea pilot, they stirred young Featherstone with romantic yarns of the sea. Long before he reached his teens, he haunted the docks of Sunderland, where he was born in 1896.

He began his apprenticeship in the Prince liners, trafficking in the Mediterranean with general cargo. At 18 he began serving as junior officer in the trans-Atlantic passenger service in the US motorships St. Paul and Philadelphia. During World War I, he was chief officer in transports conveying ammunition from England to France, being frequently bombed or chased by U-boats. At 21 he gained his master's certificate. By then he had been in most ports of the world.

Misfortune befell his first command, the freighter Alice Taylor. He was No. 13 in a convoy from Portland to the French coast and had just put out from port when the Norwegian freighter Nils rammed his ship and put a gaping hole in its bow. With his ship taking in water, Featherstone pulled her out of the line and steamed back to Portland. When he saw he couldn't make it, he ran the Alice Taylor on the beach at Weymouth.

It was this accident that helped launch Featherstone in the salvage game. Sir Frederick Young, famed mastermind of salvage in England who was then on loan to the Admiralty from the Liverpool Salvage Association, liked

113

Featherstone's presence of mind in an emergency and offered him a job.

He was to take advantage of this offer sooner than he anticipated. On her next trip out after being refloated the Alice Taylor was chased and shelled by submarines. During the chase the jinxed freighter hit a mine in the North Sea. As his ship was sinking, Featherstone herded the 21 survivors into a lifeboat and headed for shore. After battling several days and nights against severe offshore gales and huge seas, they reached shore at Yarmouth during a blinding snow storm and slumped on the beach, exhausted.

Out of the hospital and minus a ship, Featherstone reported to Sir Frederick and got a job in the Admiralty Salvage Section. One of his early assignments as a deep sea diver was the recovery of bodies from a bacon-carrying freighter which had burned and sunk near the Isle of Wight. He will never forget it. To get into the vessel, whose crew had been roasted to death after a collision with a tanker, the diving party submerged through a ventilator into the stokehold. Entering a ship's cabin, they disturbed the still waters and the bodies of four victims floated toward them "like strange wiggling ghosts." The macabre sight deranged a young officer in the diving crew. "In his excitement the poor fellow opened up his air-intake valve and his suit filled with air. We had one devil of a job getting him back up that ventilator," recalled Featherstone. "He was taken to an asylum and never dived again."

Featherstone learned the tricks of the salvage trade fast and soon was on the top rung as officer-in-charge of the Salvage Section. His most noteworthy task for the Admiralty was clearing sunken British cruisers from Zeebrugge and Ostend harbors. He worked at this from 1918 to 1921, helping raise the Vindictive, Imphegnia and Thetis. He further distinguished himself during the fire at Southampton in 1922 and supervised many other suc-

114

cessful salvage operations in British waters, among the largest being the refloating of the ex-German passenger ship Huntspill, sunk in a Southampton dock.

In the late summer of 1924, Halifax Shipyards hired him away from Liverpool Salvage and Featherstone sailed for Halifax in the salvage tug HMS Reindeer, a former gun-boat on the China station. His career on this continent has made his name a byword among mariners in all ports of the North Atlantic.

A single undertaking established Bob Featherstone's reputation as salvage expert on this side of the Atlantic. In May, 1928, the British cruiser Dauntless climbed on Thrum Cap at the entrance to Halifax harbor. Thrum Cap is a vise which seldom lets go. As master of the Reindeer, Featherstone directed the operating crew and his tug bore the brunt of the strain which eventually pulled the cruiser free. He still recalls as one of the most memorable days of his life how the Reindeer and a flotilla of tugs escorted the listing and reef-scarred Dauntless up Halifax harbor to a berth on the Dartmouth shore.

Bad luck overtook the Reindeer in 1932. She was racing to beat her rival, Foundation Franklin, to a point off Sable Island where the Hamburg American steamer Hamburg was rudderless and helpless in a severe storm. The gigantic seas opened up the Reindeer's plates and she started to sink. The Canadian Pacific Steamships liner Montcalm picked up her SOS and sped to the rescue. A daring lifeboat crew snatched Featherstone and his crew from the sinking ship with minutes to spare. The Cap made the leap into the pitching lifeboat carrying his pet Alsatian dog.

Again without a ship, Featherstone snapped up an offer from the Foundation Company to join its staff with which he has performed some of his most brilliant salvage feats. At that time the company had only one seagoing tug, the Foundation Franklin. Today Featherstone directs a powerful fleet of 25 ships, including harbor tugs, ocean-going salvage tugs, and derrick vessels. This fleet covers a wide range of sea extending from Bermuda to Newfoundland and into the St. Lawrence where Foundation recently bought out its rival, CPR's Quebec Salvage and Shipping. Since 1939 Foundation's all-weather, rough-and-tumble salvage crews have salvaged 733,718 tons of shipping. The company is well established as the largest marine salvage outfit in Canada and one of the biggest in the world.

Featherstone's skill was further illustrated when the CPS 14,000-ton freighter Beaverhill sank in Saint John harbor. Experts who had raised the Normandie from New York harbor said the New York job was child's play in comparison and wouldn't tackle it. Featherstone and his crew raised the Beaverhill in 27 months, a prodigious feat which was hampered by the treacherous Reversing Falls Rapids. On this job, he licked the problem of tides and currents by removing the ship's funnel and anchoring it to the hatch of No. 1 hold during a period of slack water. Through this makeshift tunnel, the salvage crews removed the Beaverhill's cargo of high explosives while protected from the seas. Later they raised and removed the ship itself which was a menace to navigation.

"In this business every job is different. That's why I'm so interested in it," he commented.

16

QUEEN OF THE FISHING FLEET

Louis Jaques Photo

Busy Mrs. Marie Penny directs unloading of this craft at Ramea. She knows her employees by first names.

From an office overlooking picturesque Ship's Cove in the Ramea Islands, four miles off the south coast of Newfoundland, an amiable, silver-haired business-woman named Marie S. Penny keeps loving watch over her fleet of 10 vessels, an occupation that has won her the title of Queen of the Fishing Fleet.

By ship-to-shore telephone, this energetic woman, a Newfoundlander born and bred, frequently talks to the skippers of the trawlers Senator Penny and Pennyluck as they roam the Grand Banks, to the refrigerated carrier Rameaux II en route to Boston and to all her other boats.

Fishing boats have been a part of Mrs. Penny's life for as long as she cares to remember, and today she holds more power in the islands than the all-male town council which represents the 1,000 residents.

117

Her sovereignty stems from her role as president of John Penny and Sons, Ltd., a bustling enterprise which last year alone shipped four million pounds of processed fish into the U.S. market.

Over 95 per cent of the employable people of Ramea work for the Penny company, which includes a merchandising business supplying Ramea and neighboring villages with foodstuffs and household equipment.

It is something of a family business. Mrs. Penny, whose days begin at sunrise and continue until late evening, often goes down to the wharf that fronts the modern plant, to talk to the men. She knows all of her 200 or more employees by their first names and takes an interest in their personal problems.

The flourishing business began over a century ago when a Devonshire youth named John Penny quit his job as apprentice for the port-wine House of Newman, bought a small barque and began peddling tea, molasses and flour to the outports.

Later, fired by tales of great codfish catches off Ramea, he bought out Tommy Janes, the lone inhabitant. Ever since then, "Skipper John" and his descendants have run the enterprise.

One of these descendants, George Penny, spoken of in Ramea today with a respect akin to hero-worship, became his province's first representative in the Senate when Newfoundland entered Confederation in 1949. Senator Penny's career at Ottawa was brief. He died there in December of that year.

Since then his widow, Marie, has run the business. "She drives a hard bargain," a business friend said of her, "but she's always fair."

Mrs. Penny has a daily schedule that might well tire the average captain of industry. In addition to all her business duties, she finds time to cook at her hilltop home, a 12-room, gable-roofed dwelling called the Four Winds. Her guests have included former Governor General Vincent

Massey and various skippers and their wives.

Marie Penny is not only a legend throughout Newfoundland. In 1959, for instance, she was one of 35 Canadians who dined with Queen Elizabeth and Prince Philip at a Government House banquet in Ottawa.

An inveterate traveller, she keeps close tabs on trends in the fishing industry during trips to the United States and overseas. But, says Mrs. Penny, the best part of any trip is getting back to Ramea.

In all her years of association with fishing boats, only once did she want to get away from the smell of fish — and then she regretted it.

The incident happened several years ago when Mrs. Penny, her daughter and two women companions boarded a fish-carrying boat for North Sydney. The smell was so overpowering that Mrs. Penny persuaded her companions to bunk down in a dory on deck.

In this way, they managed to dodge the worst of the smell but despite a protective tarpaulin they ended the journey covered with soot from the ship's stack and looking like miners just out of the Cape Breton pits.

With the exception of a remarkable nonagenarian and his wife, all Ramea residents live on Northwest Island, where the town of Ramea is located. Ramrod-straight "Uncle Bob" Rossiter, 90, lives a happy hermit existence with his wife on Southwest Island. The rugged outdoor type, he still gets his caribou every year and thinks nothing of trudging 14 miles over the mountains to pick berries. In earlier days he hunted seals in the Antarctic.

Among other colorful Ramea residents is Reuben Carter, 65, who once survived a full hour in frigid winter seas after being knocked overboard by a fishing craft's swinging boom.

There is no regular minister in the Anglican church, to which most of the people belong. When school is in session the teacher officiates. On non-church Sundays the men gather along the waterfront in groups known as "the Sunday morning councils" to discuss the week's events.

The people of Ramea pay no property tax. Apart from a $5 poll tax, and a $2 maximum monthly levy for a new $100,000 sewerage system, there are no civic assessments. Electricity is supplied by the Penny generating plant, the average monthly bill being $5.

The hospitable residents live in brightly painted homes and, like Mrs. Penny, think Ramea is one of the nicest spots in the world.

17

GOOD HEALTH SAILS WITH CAPT. TROAKE

National Film Board Photo

S.S. Christmas Seal calls at an outport.

Thousands of little children throughout Newfoundland and Labrador are convinced that Capt. Peter Troake, 52, the fun-loving ex-sealing master who commands the motor vessel Christmas Seal, is a personal friend of Santa Claus. They flock around the friendly, ruddy-faced Twillingate skipper when his white-hulled vessel arrives in port and listen, wide-eyed, to his weird and fanciful yarns.

Capt. Troake, a family man with three children of his own, would go to almost any lengths to keep a youngster happy. He freely admits that he and Santa are old pals. There's an ulterior motive, however, in his dockside story hours. Slyly, smack in the most exciting part of a fairy tale or a salty adventure yarn, he slips in the commercial. "Drink lots of milk, Luv," he tells the pretty little girl squatting beside him. "And you, my sons" – to a group of young boys who have gathered around – "do what Mummy says, get your rest, and I promise that I'll put in a good word for you with Santa before he comes."

An old fisherman within earshot of one of these talk-fests observed with a happy grin. "There's a wonderful lot of sense in the Captain's nonsense." Neither he nor other adults in the community would think of debunking Capt. Troake's claim that he and Santa are buddies. They know, too, that the trim little mercy ship he commands has brought them the greatest of all gifts − the prospect of health and all it can mean to happiness.

One of the most elusive craft afloat today, the Christmas Seal is operated by the Newfoundland Tuberculosis Association in its relentless war against T.B. The sleek, 104-foot vessel has twice visited each of the 1,300 communities along a 6,000-mile stretch of the rugged Newfoundland and Labrador coastline and recently began a third such voyage.

In 1947, the year this floating X-ray clinic was put into service, the number of deaths from tuberculosis in Newfoundland was 428 and the rate per 100,000 population was 127. In 1957, the number of deaths was 82 and the rate 19.2. The Christmas Seal made a major contribution to this enviable record by bringing X-ray services to isolated communities and by finding T.B. cases in the early stages.

An almost carnival-like atmosphere prevails when the vessel sails into an outport settlement. From the Christmas Seal's twin loudspeakers comes the catchy Household Brigade, a lilting, Irish two-step, or some other lively tune. As the music ends, "Ricky" Frecker, a young science student at Memorial University who doubles as the ship's disk jockey and diabetes technician, explains why the ship has come. His appeal for all persons over 21 to come aboard for X-ray examination and for those under 21 to submit to a B.C.G. scratch test usually gets a ready response.

(The initials B.C.G. are applied to an anti-tuberculosis

vaccine. They stand for Bacillus Calmet Guerin, the latter two names being those of the originators of the vaccine. In cases where there is a positive reaction to the B.C.G. skin test the patient is X-rayed to determine whether he or she has tuberculosis. Where there is a negative reaction to the B.C.G. skin test, the patient is vaccinated with the B.C.G. vaccine.)

Soon there is a steady trickle of humanity down the steep hills to the dock while others come from distant shores in dories and motorboats, all converging on the waiting vessel where Head Nurse Evelyn Watts and her staff have everything in readiness.

To the casual onlooker the scene at the dock with its milling crowd of men, women, and children might look like utter confusion. But the teamwork between the ship's crew and the nursing and medical personnel is something to see and the job rolls smoothly. There are no idle hands. Big Ches Stone, the vessel's burly first mate, dons a white smock and begins registering adults for their X-rays. Capt. Troake, Chief Engineer Ben Barbour and Second Mate Ches Bishop help direct the traffic, assist women and children aboard, and make themselves generally useful.

The children, most of whom are dressed in their Sunday best, are steered toward a cabin next to the wheelhouse on the forward deck where Nurse Ethel Saunders makes a skin test on their arms. This is to determine whether they are negative or positive reactors. On a subsequent visit, negative reactors will be vaccinated and positive cases X-rayed. In 1957 alone, B.C.G. nurses like Miss Saunders skin-tested 25,277 children and vaccinated 18,549.

Miss Saunders, who is assisted by Madonna Fagan, a student nurse, handles about 230 young patients in an average day. Her rapid-fire line of light banter usually works. "Just a pussy-cat scratch, Luv," she tells a timid child, whose fears almost always melt into relief, that the needle doesn't hurt at all. "When a young one starts to howl," she says, "they usually all start. For no good reason. For the most part they're pretty good."

Her job is not without its problems. Recently, when none of the residents of a tiny village in Placentia Bay responded to the call, Miss Saunders and Miss Fagan went to investigate. It was a windy day, the sea was rough, and occasionally a wave sprayed over the dory transporting them from ship to shore. The girls got soaked. To make matters worse, their mission was a complete failure. The villagers had religious scruples against vaccinations, X-rays and the like. They wouldn't budge. "They said it would be God's will if they got T.B," ruefully commented Miss Saunders as she arrived back dripping wet. "It wasn't God's will that I got drenched."

A considerable part of the Christmas Seal's all-important work is done aboard ship. Some is done in homes, schools and halls. Since the Department of Health began its intensive rehabilitation program in 1954, the vessel has been co-operating in a survey of the physically and mentally handicapped throughout Newfoundland. Each year, accommodation is provided on board for a rehabilitation officer working on this survey. When the accompanying photos were taken, Geraldine Chafe kept busy on this phase of the ship's many-sided program subbing for the regular officer, William Lane, who was ill. On most of her trips the Christmas Seal also carries a doctor.

While the shipboard program is in progress, Nurse Evelyn Watts, from North West River, Labrador, goes ashore to visit all known ex-tuberculosis patients. There's usually a friendly fisherman around to row her to land. In a busy day, she may walk 10 to 12 miles. A good deal of this is steep climbing. En route, she will coax those who have been tardy in responding to the opportunity to be X-rayed. Her persuasive manner usually gets results.

As Miss Watts and her colleagues have discovered, the adults don't always do what is best for the children. The mother of a seven-month-old baby, for instance, who was giving the child a slug of gin when it howled was induced to switch the formula to milk. In most cases adults in a community agree to X-ray examinations after the nurse has patiently explained they may be unwittingly exposing young children to T.B.

18

A HOUSE GOES TO SEA

Shortly after dawn one recent Saturday morning, small groups of fishermen converged on a stretch of gravel shore at Port Elizabeth island in Placentia Bay, on the south coast of Newfoundland about 45 miles due west of the huge United States naval base at Argentia. They came to help George Smith, 41, a fellow fisherman, move his home to Red Harbor, a point three miles distant on the mainland.

Smith was prepared for them. Days earlier, he had readied his two-storey, four-room, frame home for the big haul. Friendly neighbors, who hated to see him leave the island where he was born, helped him ease the building from its foundation and pull it to the water's edge over rollers liberally smeared with cod oil. All the furniture had been removed and the haulers alerted. Moving day would be whenever the wind died down and the water was calm enough to make the job possible. Today was that day. Placentia Bay has been seen in some very ugly moods. This morning the bay was as placid as a purring kitten.

House-hauling is old hat to the people of Newfoundland. In the old days it became a festive occasion. In winter the men pulled the homes over the ice, heaving on long lines and chanting native folk songs as they pulled. When they became tired they stopped for a rest and the women gave them a picnic or "mug-up" on the ice. In warmer weather, the homes were floated across the water. Always there was some fun, but never at the expense of completing the task efficiently.

In recent years some of the glamor has gone out of house-hauling. The tractor frequently takes over from the hand-line system. But there's still a considerable amount of color left. It's doubtful if many Canadians have witnessed a moving day quite like that of George Smith's.

Some of the helpers came by motor boat, others came afoot. "Boss man" Robert Smith (no relation), of Port Elizabeth, a veteran of many hauls, supervised the "launching" preparations. Two 2½ -inch tow-lines led to the sterns of two motor boats which were linked to three other motor boats. While the boats pulled, those ashore would push. A rising tide would do the rest. Such was Smith's plan.

Smith gave the "haul away!" signal at 7:25 A.M. The five motorboats gunned their engines and those ashore heaved, pried, pushed, and grunted. The house budged a foot or so and then a tow-line snapped. Within minutes it was replaced by a new line. Once again Smith gave the hauling signal. This time the house slithered over the rollers, the motor boats picked up speed and George Smith's grey clapboard home rode out into the bay amid joyous cries of "Hooray" from those ashore.

Usually the homes are floated on rafts made of empty oil drums which keep the entire structure above water. But in this case the owner figured the sea water would not seriously damage the house which had no plaster work. Within 20 minutes the house was half-submerged and from then on it was a slow drag to Red Harbor.

The entire house-hauling program in Newfoundland has been a slow drag. In March, 1956, Premier Joseph Smallwood suggested that 1,000 of the 1,300 communities scattered along Newfoundland's 6,000 coastline be scrapped. If the population were resettled in 300 large communities, the Premier said they could have such conveniences as electric lights, paved streets, more schools, doctors, nurses, hospitals, finer churches and church halls. "Isolation," the Premier declared, "is a deadening thing, a deadening thing, a paralyzing thing, a cruel thing."

Since 1950, the Smallwood government has been pushing a centralization program and in that period over 100 isolated outports have been abandoned in the move toward larger centres. In 1957, the Premier said the plan might involve moving as many as 50,000 Newfoundlanders from isolated outports. His government was prepared to offer up to $400 per family provided all the families moved to an approved location. In 1958, this grant was increased to $600.

"With this chance for financial aid, why don't more outporters jump at the chance to move?"

Weather-tanned George Senior, a neighbor of George Smith's who was in one of the lead boats looked back to see that everything was in order. "Well, in the first place, a man doesn't like to leave his home. In the second place, some of the government's relocation areas may have modern conveniences but they don't have fish which is our means of livelihood. And in the third place, many of us have built wharves and sheds and the like of that which $600 wouldn't begin to pay for if we left them behind."

By this time seven boats had joined in the laborious tow to Red Harbor. "We've had to take some wonderful chances coming across this water," said Senior. "I recall one trip coming over for the body of a woman for a funeral. She had died in Burin. We nearly didn't make it. This is as calm as I've ever seen the bay."

As the strange water cavalcade rounded the point and chugged slowly toward the shore, a small crowd had begun to gather. The most excited among them was George Smith's 32-year-old bride, Ruth, to whom the relocated home was a delayed wedding gift.

The Smiths had been married two months earlier and they had talked over the idea of moving to the mainland, weighing the pros and cons. Red Harbor won out largely on the availability of medical and hospital services, electricity, highways, and other modern advantages.

By 9:56 A.M. Ruth and George Smith's house was hard ashore at Red Harbor. Allowing for drift, it had covered the distance at about 1 m.p.h.

Then began the back-breaking work of moving the house up a 30-degree slope over a seemingly impossible pathway over which had been laid a crude sort of cribwork. This led between a henhouse and a shed after which the way was clear to the spot where the house was finally to rest — about 50 yards from the water's edge.

Friends and neighbors came from all around to lend a hand. Most of them had jobs to do but passed them up for the day to help George.

Boss man Smith formed his 40 volunteers into two lines, each pulling on heavy hawsers fitted with block and tackle. Slowly but surely they brought the house up the sharp incline, gaining sometimes less than a foot, at times only inches. There were two minor casualties. Midway up the hill they almost wrecked the henhouse. And a short time later one of the uprights near the front door of George Smith's home caught on a rock and broke away. Nothing, however, that a Newfoundland handyman couldn't fix.

At noon a halt was called for lunch and Ruth Smith helped her mother feed the hungry haulers. Then back to work. By 3:20 P.M. the job was done — just five minutes short of eight hours from the time of launching. It still had to be jacked into a level position and put into a state of proper repair but Ruth said happily: "It looks some good."

All of the men had worked gratis for a friend. But now they said their goodbyes quickly. With only half a day left, some of them had a whole day's work ahead.

19

THE ROUGH, TOUGH DAYS OF SAIL

Bottle of sand from Sable Island reminds old shipmates Lemuel   Isnor (L),   80, of Indian Point, N.S., and Capt. Rollie Knickle (R), 72, of Lunenburg, N.S., of 1927 hurricane which almost wrecked their schooner Andrava on Sable's sands.   Lloyd Heisler, center, of Andrava crew, is glad he missed the voyage.

Colorful Capt. Norman "Dynamite" Smith, 81, of Barrington Passage, N.S., recalls a long and adventurous career.

Photos by Louis Jaques

Skipper of the famed Bluenose, Capt. Angus Walters.

Capt. Titus Conrad, 77, of Riverport, N.S., sailed 22 years as master, says life of today's seamen is "heaven on earth compared to ours."

Capt. Rollie Knickle, of Lunenburg, N.S., a tall, robust sea veteran whose youthful appearance belies his 72 years, unscrewed the top from an ordinary medicine bottle and poured some of the sand it contained into the palm of his hand. "A souvenir from Sable Island," said the retired sailing master. And letting the grains sift slowly through his fingers, he told the story of a terrible ordeal at sea:

At 6 P.M. on a fateful Aug. 24, 1927, Capt. Knickle, then a husky skipper of 39, was reading in his bunk aboard the fishing schooner Andrava when Mate Lemuel Isnor of Indian Point, N.S., aroused him. Isnor was worried. "The sky looks peculiar, Captain," he said. "I think we're going to have a breeze."

Knickle went on deck for a look. The wind was coming up rapidly from the south and the sky had an ominous look. The weather had been clear when the 140-foot schooner left Canso, N.S., the day before on a routine fishing trip with a crew of 18. Now, Capt. Knickle sensed that a real storm was brewing.

The Andrava was about four miles south of the west lighthouse on Sable Island, "Graveyard of the Atlantic," where many ships had foundered. If the vessel continued on her present course, she would have to sail over 30 miles to clear the island's east bar. By sailing west, she would have to sail only 15 miles to clear the west bar. The captain lost little time in changing course.

The storm rapidly worsened. The wind increased in force and the seas became more menacing. The vessel had no radio and no engine. By 7:30 that night the wind was almost at hurricane force and the Andrava had to shorten sail. The crew took in her jib and main-sail, hoisted the storm trysail, and took two reefs in the foresail.

At 9:30 P.M., disaster nearly overtook the Andrava. A gigantic sea swept down on the pitching vessel, carrying away her storm trysail and half the jumbo. With a mighty blow it burst the foresail, broke the main gaff in three pieces and swept the dories off the deck. It also smashed the chain tackles holding the main boom, which crashed down on the cabin house and steering wheel. It washed 300 fathoms of hawser overboard.

With her steering wheel pinned beneath the boom, the schooner lay at the mercy of the sea. "Get the wheel cleared!" the captain yelled. Crew members began the difficult task of clearing the jammed wheel and by super-human effort got the boom raised and secured.

During the confusion a young crew member named Austin Knickle had gone to the vessel's bow to lower the jumbo. Just then the craft pitched suddenly, upsetting a chain locker on top of him. He cried out for help but no one heard him. The roar of the wind and the sea drowned his sobs. Half-conscious, drenched, and in severe pain, he lay pinned down for hours until his shipmates discovered his plight and freed him.

Around 11 o'clock another tremendous wave struck the Andrava and heeled her far over. Water poured down the companionways and the vessel seemed close to sinking. But she righted herself. Andrava was now perilously close to Sable. The ocean sand trap appeared to be reaching out for a new victim. Capt. Rollie took soundings. The depth was 72 to 84 feet.

We don't have much of a chance, he thought, grimly. *One more blow like that and she'll roll over.* Andrava's sails had been ripped to shreds, she was battered and leaking badly. The worried captain felt it would be suicide to continue on the present tack, with the storm abeam. He decided to take a gamble – the most daring gamble of his career. He planned to turn the Andrava and take her across the submerged Sable Island bar in the hope of reaching the north side of the island where the water was deeper and less rough. By running before the wind, there'd be less chance of capsizing. But did Andrava have enough water to clear the bar? The captain felt he had to

132

make the attempt and explained his plan to the crew. "I'll need a volunteer to lash himself to the wheel," he said.

Isnor quickly responded. As shipmates lashed him to the wheel so that he wouldn't be washed overboard, Isnor promised them, "If the Lord lets me stay here, I'll sail her across."

It was now midnight and the storm was at its peak. The wind, now roaring at 75 miles per hour, had stirred up gigantic seas. Running before the gale, Andrava began to cross the bar in great lurches. Each huge wave lifted her, then plunged her down till her keel grazed the sandy bottom. But each time she struck, another wave lifted her free.

Now Andrava's deck was a fury of flying spray and sand. Through it all the courageous Isnor kept a tight grip on the wheel, his vision almost blotted out. Some of the crew members had lashed themselves to the pumps as they worked desperately to keep the vessel afloat. Most of the men prayed and some cursed the sea. Each plunge toward the sandy bottom might be the vessel's last. Few ships had ever touched on Sable and escaped. Capt. Knickle prayed that the wind wouldn't change and drive them back on the bar.

After harrowing minutes that seemed like hours, Andrava moved more easily. She was across the bar, heading into deeper and calmer waters. By 3 A.M., Capt. Knickle and his crew could hear the seas breaking behind them and the storm began to moderate. At daylight the crew started to haul in the hawser. This huge mass of heavy rope, which had dragged astern of the schooner after being swept overboard, had kept some of the high seas from breaking over Andrava, and acting as a sea-anchor, had helped steersman Isnor. The crew repaired what was left of the sails as the schooner headed back to land.

"It was at this point," related Capt. Knickle, "that

we noticed the deck was covered with sand. I put some of it in this bottle. We were lucky to come out of it alive. We arrived in Lunenburg at 1 A.M., Sept 29, and put our one seriously injured man in hospital."

Nothing like this hurricane had hit the Nova Scotia coast in half a century. Practically the entire fishing fleet was at sea when it struck and hundreds lost their lives. Nothing was ever heard of the Nova Scotia schooners Sadie E. Knickle, Mahala, Clayton Walters, Joyce M. Smith, Sylvia Mosher, or Uda A. Corkum which were lost with their entire crews. Scores of smaller vessels were driven ashore. The United States schooner Columbia, which had raced with the Bluenose in 1923, went down off Sable Island.

Bluenose herself was fishing at the time and on several occasions reeled so far over in the heavy seas that her sheer poles lay in the water. She was badly battered but her sturdy timbers and skillful handling saw her safely through.

It is a tribute to the sailing skill of Capt. Angus Walters and his crew that Bluenose survived storms at sea to become five times winner of the International Schooner Races. Capt. Walters, a sharp-witted old sea dog of 79 who is perhaps the best known of all Nova Scotia sailing masters, today runs a dairy on the shore of Lunenburg harbor within a ship's length of the sea he so dearly loves. He's a busy man but is always ready to argue, preferably about politics, with the same vigor with which he battled storms at sea.

Sailing masters like Capt. Knickle and Capt. Walters are products of a hard school. As one veteran sailor put it, "In the days of sail it was always a word and a blow. And the first blow always counted." Some of the mates were exceptionally tough.

Such a man was the first mate of the Yarmouth full-rigged schooner Jane Burrill. Capt. Fred R. Currier, 87, of Yarmouth, still has painful memories of this bully. At

4 o'clock one morning the mate sent him to get brooms to scrub the deck. Currier was then 15 and a deck boy. Hurrying to obey the mate's order, he failed to notice that the hold had been left uncovered. Currier plunged into the opening and fell 20 feet, landing across the inner keel. The boy was still unconscious when a crew member found him four hours later.

When Currier came round in his bunk, he was aching all over. The mate came in. He was mad because Currier hadn't returned to scrub the deck.

"Get out of that bunk! There'll be no shamming on this ship!" he roared.

The aching and dazed youngster scrambled out of his bunk and staggered to the deck.

"Go up there and overhaul the maintopsail spillin' lines!"

In all his seafaring career this was one of the toughest orders he had ever been called on to obey. His hands were too weak to support his weight so he had to elbow his way into the shrouds. Laboriously, he made the painful climb and crawled out on the topsail yard.

Fortunately the sea was calm, and somehow Currier managed to do the job and return to the deck safely.

Despite experiences like this, Currier has many happy memories of the sea, particularly of his days in sailing ships. Like most of these hardy sea veterans, he has a deep affection for the ocean, though he does not hesitate to call it a "vile-tempered old hell cat."

Capt. Norman "Dynamite" Smith, 81, of Barrington Passage, N.S., has the same attitude. After more than half a century of sailing he still loves to talk of the days of sail and when he first went to sea as a boy of 15.

A veteran of three wars – the Boer War, World War I and World War II – Smith must have had his own personal guardian angel watching over him during his adventurous career. A self-styled "old pirate," he acquired the nickname "Dynamite" by making 42 crossings of the Atlantic in World War I in ships filled with TNT — without the protection of convoys.

In World War II he gained a further nickname, "Iceberg," for establishing a series of weather stations in the frigid North Atlantic zone for the United States government. He also ferried troops, munitions and supplies across the ocean when the Battle of the Atlantic was at its height.

One hazy night in May, 1942, Capt. Smith was piloting the 3,000-ton freighter Sonia from New York to join a convoy at Halifax when his ship was torpedoed 40 miles off Seal Island, N.S., with the loss of 11 of her 48-man crew. As the vessel started to sink, Smith ordered her flag raised and the lifeboats lowered.

The survivors had barely rowed away from the sinking ship when a Nazi submarine broke the surface nearby and its deck guns were quickly trained on the lifeboat. With a magnificent show of disdain, Smith turned toward his shipmates and directed them as they broke into There'll Always Be An England.

Smith said later, "We thought our number was up." But the Nazis held their fire.

"What ship was that?" the sub commander called out.

"The Sonia," Smith answered.

"What cargo?"

"General."

"What destination?"

"Sorry. I haven't got my orders yet."

"Is everything all right? Do you know where you you are?"

When Capt. Smith replied, "Yes," the U-boat's crew climbed into the conning tower and the craft submerged. Two days later the weary survivors reached shore at Seal Island.

During one of his troop-carrying voyages, Capt. Smith, whose vocabularly included a number of words not taught in Sunday school, had a brush with some of the U.S. Army high brass. He had completely forgotten the incident by the time he returned to New York. Then he was summoned before an admiral.

"A serious complaint has been lodged against you, Capt. Smith, by a colonel in the United States Army," said the Admiral.

The Bluenose skipper raised his eyebrows in a look of genuine surprise. "Oh," he asked, "What did I do?"

"According to Col. ————, you told him to get the hell off your bridge or you'd put him on the first big rock you came to." Reading from the complaint sheet, the admiral quoted the indignant colonel's version of his tangle with Smith. The language was strong, forceful and to the point.

As he listened to the charge, the puzzled look faded from Capt. Smith's wrinkled features. "I still don't remember the incident, Admiral," he commented. "But that sure sounds like me!"

The admiral reprimanded the captain for his conduct, but only half-heartedly.

Today, Capt. Smith lives the enforced role of land-lubber. He and his wife have an attractive home beside a beautiful flower garden and a pond containing a ship model and seven ducks. His room is built like the cabin of a ship and he is surrounded by pictures and souvenirs of his life on the sea.

Memories are dear to all these old salts, and the memories of a stormy passage from Cardiff, Wales, to Bremerton Navy Yard near Seattle in the big, three-masted sailing ship Scottish Locks still linger in the mind of Capt. George Parry, of Digby, N.S., more than half a century later. It was in 1906, before the Panama Canal was completed, and the vessel had to sail around Cape Horn, notorious for its bad weather.

"I sailed around the Horn six or seven times in my career and it was always rough going," Capt. Parry related. "But this trip in 1906 was the worst I ever experienced. I was serving as second mate. We took an awful beating from the wind and sea. For three solid weeks we were blown over 300 to 400 miles of ocean without making an inch of progress in the direction we wanted to go. We finally made it and when we got to Seattle it took a month in the shipyard to repair the damage."

Today, in retirement, this big, friendly skipper lives with his wife and daughter, Mavis, six, just outside Digby. Parry, who is in his seventies, is one of the comparatively few Canadians who is drawing both the family allowance and the old-age pension.

In an adventure-packed life at sea, he rose all the way from ordinary seaman before the mast to commodore of the Canadian Pacific Steamships' fleet. He was captain of the 42,500-ton Empress of Britain, the largest ship ever commanded by a Nova Scotian or any Canadian. The ship was torpedoed in World War II.

As a gunnery officer with the rank of lieutenant in the Royal Navy, he served in H.M.S. Vanguard and saw action in the Battle of Jutland during World War I. In November, 1919, after nearly seven years of service in the Royal Navy, he joined the C.P.S. as a first officer and remained with the company until his retirement in January, 1945, after serving ashore as the line's general superintendent.

One of the busiest periods in Capt. Parry's career came during World War II when he was assistant director in the shipping division of the Department of Transport. At times he had as many as five big Atlantic liners at the Halifax sea wall at one time – discharging, loading cargo and putting troops aboard. Like others on this important job he would work for days with little more than a catnap on a bench in the dockside office.

Capt. Parry first went to sea when he was 16 and while still in his teens was making round-the-world voyages in square-riggers. "Those days," he says, "were the happiest ones of my life."

In the days of sail a man had to be a jack of many

trades and if he was an acrobat it helped. Parry still recalls a task he was given while serving as second officer in a cargo ship bound from Calcutta to Bombay with a load of coal in the summer of 1909. A gaping hole was accidentally punched in the vessel's forepeak by the anchor as it was being raised. The damage was above the waterline and the passage might have been uneventful, but a storm came up in the Bay of Bengal and the vessel started to take in water.

At the captain's order, the crew rigged up a "pudding" (a makeshift plug of wood and canvas) to fill the hole and keep out the water. One end of a rope was tied to the pudding, the other to a long stick. The plan was to push the stick through the hole from the outside of the ship and then draw it in, pulling the pudding against the hole to plug it and seal out the sea.

The trick was to get the stick through the hole from the outside so that it could be pulled up from within. Parry, then a young man of 25, drew the assignment. As the ship pitched and tossed in the mounting seas, shipmates lowered him over the side in a bos'n's chair. For more than an hour he struggled at the perilous job, being hoisted up by crewmates as the ship dived into the sea, swinging into the ship's side when she came up – all the time trying to push the stick through the hole. Parry estimates he made more than 100 attempts before he got the stick in the target and was pulled aboard, drenched and exhausted. Happily, the pudding served its purpose and the crew were able to pump the ship comparatively free of water.

Tall, lean Capt. Titus Conrad, 77, of Riverport, N.S., who sailed 22 years as master, recalls a similar instance aboard the schooner Harold Conrad in July, 1922. Around 11 o'clock on a foggy night about 22 miles from St. John's an English barquentine rammed them on their port side and tore off the schooner's rigging. It also opened up a hole in the Harold Conrad's side and she started to ship water.

Young Harold Mosher, of Riverport, was lowered over the side to make repairs. He had a piece of canvas smeared with tar to slap over the hole and strips of wood to nail on this to secure it.

Time and again the young seaman's head would go under when a wave would strike before his mates could pull him clear. But at last, he achieved the seemingly impossible and the schooner made port safely.

"The modern seaman has radar, depth sounders, all sorts of navigational aids," commented Capt. Conrad. "It's heaven on earth compared to what we had."

Yet almost all the veterans who sailed under both sail and steam say they preferred the former. Commented one elderly captain, "You can't stand in the way of progress but, personally, I liked the old sailing vessel. It was a hard life. But it was a man's world. There are too many luxuries today."